PERFECT LOVE

God's Battle Plan for the Broken...
and the Brokenhearted

Brian Peart

Participating Editors
Brice Nelms & Bill Prince

PUBLISHED *by* PARABLES
Earthly Stories with a Heavenly Meaning

PERFECT LOVE
God's Battle Plan for the Broken... and the Brokenhearted

Copyright © Brian Peart
2018

Published By Parables
January, 2018

Unless otherwise specified Scripture quotations are taken from the New American Standard Bible.

ISBN 978-1-945698-41-5
Printed in the United States of America

Readers should be aware that Internet Web sites offered as citations and/or sources for further information may have been changed or disappeared between the time this was written and when it is read.

PERFECT LOVE

God's Battle Plan for the Broken...
and the Brokenhearted

Brian Peart

Participating Editors
Brice Nelms & Bill Prince

 PUBLISHED *by* PARABLES
Earthly Stories with a Heavenly Meaning

"There is no fear in love, but perfect love casts out fear"

1 John 4:18

FOREWORD

Yes, Jesus came to pay the price for our sins. That was His big picture vision and purpose for being here. But he accomplished it by focusing on a few prongs which He proclaimed in Luke 4:18, "The Spirit of the Lord is upon me, because He has anointed me to preach the gospel to the poor, he has sent me to proclaim release to the captives, and recovery of sight to the blind, to set free those who are oppressed." If you read the Gospel accounts of Jesus' life, this is exactly what He did. Every day He got up, prayed, and walked out to preach the gospel, heal the sick and set people free. He had his big vision of what He was here for (the Cross), but He just focused on the few big things He was gifted and called to do and then each day just did those things to whoever was put in front of Him. We never see Him rush. He was never in a hurry but always on time, and we can follow His lead. We can focus the big picture of our life on Him, begin to move in the main areas that are uniquely given to us and do the next step God gives us as each day unfolds. It is exciting to wake up and know that God may be up to something big that day and all you need to do is just obey. He says His yoke is easy and His burden is light. By letting Him direct the steps, the entire universe is at His disposal to bring things into your life that you could never imagine. All you have to worry about is the few things YOU have already been gifted or blessed with. So let's go ahead and work on YOUR big picture battle plan. It begins by starting where you are...

Table of Contents

Prologue:

A Pivotal Moment

I came into the room and there she was, as beautiful as ever, seated on the couch in one corner of the room, the counselor in a chair in the opposite corner about five feet away. The counselor was a Christian counselor named Dottie, referred by my friend and mentor Bill Prince.[1] She was a little older, though I would not want to guess the age. She seemed mild mannered. Think Aunt Bea from the Andy Griffith show for those who can recollect back that far, but she had a great knack for cutting through the excuses we often use to block us and very sweetly call us out, an annoying and wonderful quality. I would grade her a good counselor. And yes, we were there for marriage counseling.

My ex-wife is 5'3" and is, in my opinion, stunningly

---

1   Bill Prince is the Executive Minister of Biblical Principles, Inc., a 501(c)(3) religious organization. You may personally reach him by emailing him at info@biblicalprinciplesinc.org.

gorgeous. 45 years old but she looks 28. Her hair is blonde with highlights and her eyes are tough to describe. Auburn might be the closest you can get but that really does not do them justice. Different hues of brown come together in a glorious display and her smile has a way of melting a heart. She was the great love of my life. I had never loved any woman up to that point the way I loved her. She opened up parts of my heart I did not know even existed. She was my world.

Our courtship was like a fairy tale. We met and were smitten with each other. Within one month, I told her I loved her. Within three, I was picking out rings. In month four, I asked her to marry me on the beach at sunrise and by six months we were walking down the aisle. I never felt so complete. To this day she says it was the only time she was truly happy in her entire life.

And yet, here we were in marriage counseling just four years later. She had been living at her mom's house after moving out two months prior, stating she wanted a divorce. It took me two months to get her to agree to go to counseling. I finally won that battle and here we were. Love doesn't make a marriage last. Commitment does. Along the way, her commitment waned and I wanted desperately to know why. I was hoping the counseling would uncover that piece for us. I knew she still loved me, and I was head over heels for her still, so why were we here? What happened in that counseling session and the ensuing few months drove me deeper into the Word of God and opened up the journey that ultimately led to the writing of this book.

We started the session off with prayer, and then dove into the discussion. I thought we were going to discuss how she had kissed another man, or had moved out and wanted a divorce without even really trying to make it work. She had just quit trying and I wanted to know why. Shockingly, the focus instead was on me and the way my criticism had caused her to shut down. I was just floored that they were "teaming up" on me but I accepted what I felt was their criticism and decided to dive deeper into this matter. Divorce still takes two and there is no doubt I was partly to blame. If I could improve myself somehow to try to make this work, I was going to do it. The word they used was controlling, that I was a control freak. I went home after that session and decided I needed to get to the bottom of it.

As I began to study what makes someone controlling, the overwhelming thing that I found was that FEAR is the heart of what drives a control freak. It could be fear of losing control or any number of things, but at the end of the day, fear is the main driving force behind those who would be labeled controlling. If you are hurting, if you are scared, if you are unsure, then it is likely FEAR is a root cause of the problem. Fear can take on many forms; you can have the fear of being alone, of being rejected, of being not good enough, and there can be many other manifestations. I decided to go to Scripture to root out this problem and see if indeed, fear was limiting me. So I went to the Bible, which is my ultimate source of instruction and wisdom, looking for fear and how to overcome it. There I found this passage from 1 John 4:18, **"There is no fear in love, but perfect love casts out fear."** I knew then I had to dive into the Love of God, dig deep into His word and learn this lesson deeply...the rest of this book is a result of that study.

Every one of us has pivotal moments in our lives that we can look back and point to as a key moment that marked a shift or a change. My divorce and the accompanying learning was one of those moments for me. Sometimes these moments are planned but most of the time they are thrust upon us. Some crisis or disruption forces us to look deep within ourselves and find a different course. Some people do quit when they hit those moments. They never recover. But some take those moments, learn the deep lessons, and rise to greater things. My hope is you are that second type. We learn more in the valleys. If you are broken or brokenhearted, you are not alone and it does not matter how you got here. The information I am about to share is straight from God's Word and His wisdom can change your life if you let it. This can be your moment! So let's dive in to perfect love and find out how to rise to our higher high!

Chapter 1:

Accepting God

Don't be confused by the title. I am NOT talking about accepting Jesus Christ into your heart as your Lord and Savior. That is a different matter altogether. I am assuming that those reading this have already nailed down that salvation decision. This book is written for Christians. If you are not a Christian, much of what I share with you will not have an impact. IF YOU ARE NOT SURE OF YOUR SALVATION, I invite you to put this book down and nail that piece today. Go to your pastor, go to a strong Christian friend or family member, or call this ministry, Biblical Principles. My good friend and mentor Bill Prince will be glad to discuss this with you. His email is info@ biblicalprinciplesinc.org. Bill is as solid as it gets. He has taught me so much and can really help you secure your salvation. Tell him I sent you.

Now that we have that taken care of, let's dive into the real heart of this chapter which is God's love and acceptance of you, right now, just as you are. When I realized that fear was the heart of my problem and that perfect love casts out fear, I decided to look up everywhere the word LOVE is used in the Bible and use my Strong's Concordance to look up the original Hebrew and/or Greek translation. The Strong's Concordance is a large reference book that cross references each word in the Bible with its corresponding original Hebrew or Greek meaning. Many times, the original meaning of the words give more understanding of the passage and hence, more insight into God and His character. So, I grabbed my concordance and my Bible and began.

The word LOVE or some form of it (loved, lovingkindness), shows up 547 times in Scripture. That kind of surprised me. I thought it was a lot more. By contrast, the word Lord appears over 14,000 times and the word God also appears thousands of times. God is love. He is the author of love, but He is MUCH MORE than love. Love is just one aspect of God's character. Yet, our misunderstanding of love, of God, can have big ramifications on our lives. **How you see God is how you view the world. It shapes how you deal with things and how you "walk" with the Lord. Even the way we operate and communicate flows from our understanding of God and how we see Him.** Many times, this goes back to our earthly father and we form a view of God by our view of how our earthly father is or was.

For example, my earthly father was sort of disappointed in me. I had Asperger's Syndrome when I was young, although back in the 60's that was never diagnosed. It led me to being quite different than other kids initially and that was a source of embarrassment for my dad. Growing up in New Jersey, we went to a Catholic church part of the time and a Lutheran church part of the time (mom was Catholic, dad was Lutheran), and I never really heard much about a deep relationship with God. Church was more ritual. It seemed to me to be rules, more like do's and don'ts. Even prayers were ritualized. We would repeat the Lord's prayer. That was kind of my background "canvas" by which I viewed God and church. I really felt like my relationship with the Lord did not start until I was thirty, that is when I asked the Lord into my heart and got baptized.

Initially, I saw God as a disapproving father. In hindsight, I can see why based on my background. I viewed God as a judging father who rewarded me when I did good but punished me when I did bad. I knew He loved me, and I loved Him, but I constantly felt like God was looking down on me in disappointment as the little sins that crept into my life, like sinful thoughts, were front and center in my quiet time. I remember praying and then sinful thoughts would interrupt my prayers and I would beat myself up over my weakness. I felt shame very often and strove very hard to be good so I could please the Lord. This had obvious results in my real life and my quiet time. I felt the constant pressure to "work" for the Lord and to be "perfect as my heavenly father is perfect." Maybe you see God in that way as well...well I have good news.

Yes, God is a righteous judge, and we will suffer consequences from our actions. However, he is also a merciful Lord and always forgiving if we turn to Him and repent. Later, after a major tragedy forced me to go VERY deep into the Word, I discovered that God does not look down on me with a frown. He looks down and sees the beautiful sinless Son of Man. He sees Jesus and His atoning blood. He looks down and smiles on me. That thought blew me away. It changed how my quiet time was and allowed me to release the past of my childhood and embrace His love. That opened me up to more love in my personal life. And that opened me up to be ready for the next phase. Once you understand that God is not disappointed with you constantly, that you don't have to WORK to earn His love, it is just freely given, you can be ready to freely love others. Had I not uncovered this truth, I would not have been ready for a love like my ex-wife's. BUT EVEN THAT VIEW OF GOD'S LOVE IS ONLY ONE ASPECT OF HIS LOVE. As I was about to discover in my quiet time after this most recent tragedy and divorce, God's love is so much more.

As I began my study of love, I found the first time the word was used in Scripture was in Genesis chapter 22:2. "Take your son, your only son Isaac, whom you **_love,_** and go to the land of Moriah and offer him there as a burnt offering." Here, the Hebrew word used is **_"ahab"_** which means "have affection for or like (sexually or otherwise)."[2] It seems to correspond with the way we most often use love to love something or like someone greatly. Whether we love one another or love a thing, we use the word love almost casually. It seems the Hebrews did as well. In Genesis 27:4, the next time the word is used, we find Isaac telling Jacob to "make me a savory dish of meat the type that I *love*." Much as we would say we love pizza or some dish. The same root word *"ahab"* is used.

In Genesis 29:20, we see a slightly different version of love used in the Hebrew language. The Bible says, "So Jacob served seven years for Rachel and they seemed to him as just a few days because of his love for her." Here, the root Hebrew word is *"ahabah"* which is a feminine form of the word ahab but means the same thing – affection or love. It seems like this slight variation would be most like the way we say we are "in love" with someone.

Usually when we see the word love in the Old Testament, it is some form of these two words UNTIL WE GET TO DEUTERONOMY 7:7. Here the Bible says this, "The Lord did not set his *love* on you nor choose you because you were more in number than any of the peoples, for you were the fewest of the peoples." Here the Hebrew word is *"chashaq."* It is a prime root and it means "to cling to or join" and to "delight in, to have a delight in, to desire long for, or set in long for, or set in love."[3] WOW.

2   James Strong, *Strong's Concordance: Bible Dictionary* (P.T.L. Television Network, 1975).
3   Ibid

This thought stopped me in my tracks. The Lord God, the Creator of Heaven and Earth, DELIGHTS in me. Not in some future me, not in my best me, but he delights in me RIGHT NOW, just as I am. He set His love on me and wants me to cling to Him. He longs for me. Desires me. And He feels that way about YOU. He delights in YOU. Think about this for a minute. Let this thought sink into you. He delights in YOU. Right now, just as you are. Not some future you, but you RIGHT now. And He is DELIGHTED in what He sees. WHAT A WORD!

I think of the way we look at a toddler that is just starting to try to learn how to walk. He totters, then falls, then struggles up to his feet and falls again. He holds onto a coffee table for support and then lets go and takes a step and falls. We watch and we clap and we are excited and it is beautiful. This baby is falling down, literally failing, again and again, yet it is wonderful to us! We delight in the struggle. There is no criticism or condemnation for the failure. Just encouragement to get up and try again. We know that this struggle is part of life and soon enough, walking will be easy for the toddler. There is so much love there for that little child of ours, for the beautiful struggle. We take pictures. We video. We put it on Instagram and Facebook and everyone collectively goes, "ahhhh." It is delightful in our site. Joyful…GOOD!

We are that toddler to God. We get up. We stumble. We fall. We get up and try again. And fail. And again. And God is looking down with joy! This thought is too overwhelming to me. God looks at my little heart, my little struggle, my failure like we look at our toddler trying to walk. No condemnation, just joy. Just love. "What is man that you are mindful of him" (Psalm 8:4). David got it. David was said to be a man after God's own heart and I think that is partly because he understood this piece. The Chris Tomlin song has the line, "You know the depths of my heart and you love me the same...you are amazing God." [4] He knows your insecurity, and He loves you just as you are. That doesn't mean He wants you to stay there any more than we want that toddler to stay crawling the rest of their life. We love them, just as they are, even with their struggle.

God accepts you. He accepts you. He accepts me. Just as we are, even falling down over and over. What a glorious thought. Do you realize how important you are to Jesus? He cares about every aspect of your life. Every tear, every sorrow. He loves you. I encourage you to take a minute now, put down this book, close your eyes...and imagine. Just think of how much love the parent has for the toddler trying to walk for the first time. If you are a parent, think of the first time your first child was trying to walk. Think of the excitement and joy and love even with the falling down. You were filming it, telling friends. It was an awesome time in your life. Now visualize yourself as that toddler, God as that parent. Feel the joy, hear Jesus Himself clapping for you, the excitement that God has for

---

4   Chris Tomlin, *Indescribable* (Capitol Christian Music Group, 2004).

you…feel His love wash over you…feel the energy, the joy, the gladness of a Father who loves you JUST AS YOU ARE. Even amidst your failures, you won't fall out of His love. Wow! Makes me cry thinking about it even as I write this. WOW!

In Psalm 23, David penned these words:

"The Lord is my shepherd, I shall not want. He makes me lay down in green pastures; He leads me beside still waters; He restores my soul. Even though I walk through the valley of the shadow of death, I fear no evil, for YOU ARE WITH ME!"

Let Him restore your soul. The first step in moving from brokenhearted to victory is understanding that even though you are in a valley, whether you are in the valley because of your actions or just because of life, GOD IS WITH YOU. He is there. He is not disappointed. He is not upset. He is looking at you lovingly. He gets pain. He gets suffering. Whatever you are going through, He understands and He loves you just the same. Close your eyes…feel His Joy washing over you. KNOW that He accepts you just as you are. Let this Perfect Love fill your mind and heart and you will find your fear disappearing. Perfect Love casts out fear, remember? He is with you, in the valley, there is NOTHING to fear. "I will fear no evil for God is with me!" Take some time, dwell on this wonderful thought. Journal it. Write down what God is showing you. Write down this powerful verse. Perfect love casts out fear. Read

Psalm 23 and let the truth of His love wash over you.

The first step to going from brokenhearted to victory is understanding God's Accepting love. He accepts you. He doesn't see you as a failure. He is not disappointed in you. He loves you right where you are. He frees you with that love. And you are free to accept others this same way. Love them as God loves you. Once we understand that God accepts us as we are, once we have this peace in our hearts, we can move beyond fear to the next step in the battleplan...Accepting YOUR Glory!

My Thoughts on Chapter 1:

Chapter 2:

Accepting Your Glory

I'm big on visualizing things. It is one thing for me to write down ideas and thoughts but if you can close your eyes and visualize the idea and grasp the thought, you can REALLY learn it. Know it, and it can become a part of you and in this case, a part of your healing.

I have another exercise for you. Close your eyes and visualize the most beautiful thing in nature you have ever seen. A sunrise on a beach, a sunset on a meadow, a field of sunflowers, a majestic mountain range, a quiet meadow, a peaceful lake. Think of the most beautiful place you know, the most amazing place in nature you have ever seen. A place that takes your breath away and almost demands the gasp, "Thank you God." The place where you can't help but feel close to God and almost thank Him for the beauty He has poured out on you in that moment. Do you have it? Can you see it?

Now think of this. You are GREATER and MORE magnificent to God than that place! You are MORE glorious than the most beautiful sunrise or sunset. The mountain lake, the quiet stream, all of it is good. But you are VERY good. You are greater even than the most beautiful place in the world. Whoa! In Genesis 1 is the story of creation. God made light, seas, land and all the creatures of this world. He created everything and decreed it was good (Genesis 1:25). Then in verse 26, He makes man. Let's pick up the story there…

"Then God said, 'let us make man in our image, according to Our likeness. Let them have dominion over the fish of the sea, over the birds of the air, and over the cattle, over all the earth and over every creeping thing that creeps on the earth.'" So God created man in His own image, in the image of God. He created them, male and female. "God blessed them and God said to them, 'be fruitful and multiply, fill the earth and subdue it, have dominion over the fish of the sea, over the birds of the air, and over every living thing that moves on the earth.'" Genesis Chapter 1 ends with this beautiful statement in verse 31, "Then God saw everything that He had made, and indeed it was VERY good." After each part of creation, God looked and saw that it was good. After He made the land and all its mountains, He claimed it was good. After He made the beautiful sunsets and sunrises, He said it was good. After He made the most beautiful of creatures, He said it was good. Only after He made man, the pinnacle of His creation, did He look out and call it VERY good. We are greater even than the most beautiful place in nature you have ever seen. Greater than the mountains, the sea, the sun. More magnificent. Grand. Awesome. The words go on.

Not only that, but we alone were made after God's own image. In Genesis 1:26 God said, "Let Us make man in Our image, according to Our likeness." Some may have you believe that we were evolved from monkeys, but the Bible clearly says it is not so. Well over 100 years after Darwin proposed that ridiculous theory, it still is a theory because it just cannot be proven. Species evolve but they do not transmutate. No species has EVER evolved into another species...PERIOD! At the end of the day, ONLY man can plan a vacation, think about his existence, read a book like this and plan a future. That is not something that has evolved. That is something given specifically to you and me by a sovereign God. It is our deity, our spirit. It is what makes us human. Special. We were uniquely and divinely created in the image of God.

Psalm 139:14 claims probably the greatest truth ever written, that we are "fearfully and wonderfully made." I encourage you to stop right now and read Psalm 139. It is beautiful. In Psalm 139: 13-16, David writes about the truth of our creation, the glory of it all.

"For You formed my inward parts. You wove me in my mother's womb. I will give thanks to You, for I am fearfully and wonderfully made. Wonderful are your works and my

soul knows it very well. My frame was not hidden from you when I was made in secret and SKILLFULLY wrought in the depths of the earth; Your eyes have seen my unformed substance and in Your book were all written the days that were ordained for me, when as yet there was not one of them."

Not only were you specially made by the hand of a loving God, unique and unlike any other, He has already seen all your days from birth up to now, and God knows all your days going forward. He thinks about you constantly. Doesn't that blow you away? David writes in Psalm 139: 17-18, "How precious also are Your thoughts to me O God! How vast is the sum of them! If I should count them, they would outnumber the sand." God not only made you unique. He not only knows the times you have had and the times to come. He thinks about you, cares about you. He knows when you lie down and when you get up. You can't run from Him. You can't hide. He loves you. He sees your innermost parts, and He loves you! You are unique and beautiful. You are made in the very image of GOD! WOW!

And it is not just the Old Testament that claims these truths about us being made after God's own image. The New Testament talks about believers being a new creation in Christ and being made into His image. In Ephesians 4:24 we read, "and put on the new self, which in the *likeness of God* has been created in righteousness and holiness of truth." In Colossians 3:10 we read, "put on the man who is renewed in knowledge according to the <u>image of Him</u> who created him."

In Christ, we are a new man or woman, made in the image of God. Old Testament or New, the same statement rings true. We were made in the image of an amazing God and as such we are amazing! We need to embrace this glory if we are to move on to the next phase of healing. Embrace the fact that God, "made him (man) a little lower than God, and you crown him with glory and majesty!" (Psalm 8:5).

And reader, the maker of the heavens chose YOU. Deuteronomy 7:6 says, "I have chosen you." Adrian Rogers is someone whose preaching and teaching impacted many of my heroes. He wrote something about this truth in a little book entitled, *The Wonder of It All*. I want to share it with you. He writes, "You are uniquely and divinely created. You are chosen to be a co-heir with the Son of God to the glories and riches of heaven. What a wonderful salvation is yours! Have you ever wondered when you became so special to Him? It was in the counsel halls of eternity. It was before He swung this world into space. You were on His heart before anything was. You are special, like none other. What a humbling thought to know that we were in the heart and the mind of God before the foundation of this world! God is for us!"[5]

---

5   Adrian Rogers, Tom Fox, *The Wonder of It All* (B&H Publishing Group, 2001).

Do you get it? Do you see it? You need to understand these truths before we can move on to the next chapter. Before we can form a plan and sculpt your future. You may have started this book brokenhearted, steeped in perceived failure. Maybe it is a divorce or problems with your kids or your job or your income. Maybe the failure was a personal one. When those times happen, it is normal to be down. But the Cross has made you flawless. Right now, go in prayer and ask God once and for all to forgive you from this past. You are RELEASED FROM IT. Put it away, right now, forever and rise up to your new glorious time. Go to God. Ask Him to forgive all of it. Name the sins individually. Cry, it's okay. Take it to Him and release it and know, just like that toddler, that this was just a fall. No matter how bad things have gotten, the past is behind you. Time to grab that coffee table, pull yourself up, and take another step!

Have you released it? Don't continue until you nail the past once and for all, get on your knees and ask Him to forgive you and He will. He promises it. "If my people, who are called by my name, will humble themselves and pray and seek my face and turn from their wicked ways, then I will hear from heaven and I will forgive their sin" (NIV, 2 Chronicles 7:14). It is gone. You are clean. He has cast that sin as far away from you as the East to the West. He has forgiven and more than that, He has forgotten! "Therefore, there is now no condemnation for those who are in Christ Jesus" (Romans 8:1). He won't condemn you. He won't bring it up again! So release it to Him, and rise up, clean and free at last!

We must understand these truths. God accepts and delights in us right where we are, and He has made us unique and special. You are more than where you are at, more than where you have been. You are that toddler, but you are getting up. And God delights in it. He has a plan for you and it is a beautiful plan. Are you ready for it? If you truly grasp the truth that He accepts you, you are ready to put aside the hurt and pain and grasp this other amazing truth, that you were chosen by God and are more beautiful than the most glorious sunset. You are ready to move on. God accepts and delights in you. You are glorious and special. If you believe these truths, deep down in your heart, then you are ready for God's higher high. Let's begin to move past the pain to your glorious new future.

My Thoughts on Chapter 2:

Chapter 3:

How to Move Past the Pain

So you know God accepts you as you are and you know that you are fearfully and wonderfully made, right? You have asked Him to forgive you and you are clean. So you are ready to go, hit the ground, take on the battle and rejoice for ever more, right? These truths alone should be sufficient to infuse you with energy; however, if you are honest or like most people, doubt and fear still linger. Why?

Habits have formed, negative habits, and it takes 21-30 days to break a habit. This book has not even taken you one day to read to this point. Most people have a horrible habit of looking at the 10% that is wrong and not the 90% that is right. And when I say most people, I am talking like 90+% of the population who spend most of their time worrying about the things wrong instead of embracing the things that are right. I have fallen into that trap many times myself. If you had stage four terminal cancer and only three days to live you would beg for the problems you have right now. Yet we throw things like our health, the love we have in our lives, cars, homes, etc aside to focus on this little thing or that little thing that is not right. We are bombarded by commercials, pushing the same message that something is missing, but if you get our product, life will be better.

And though intellectually we know material things are not where true happiness is found, it is a horrible human condition to focus on what is lacking instead of focusing on God and His glorious truths. The way to move past these bad habits and focus on God's truths is by creating a new habit of focusing on what God has said about you. You can create this by writing down what I call a "mantra." This is a one paragraph or even a one page document that claims God's truths about yourself and Him and then repeating it morning and night. If you repeat truths every day, right before you go to bed and when you first wake up, you will begin to train your subconscious mind. The subconscious mind cannot discern fact or fiction. It just hears what it is told, and if you tell it something over and over again, it will believe it as fact. And the best time to impact this mind is right before bed and right when you wake up in the morning. If you repeat this mantra consistently, every morning and night for 21 days, you will begin to embrace and accept what is written on it. Your subconscious mind will then begin to get to work incorporating these truths into your life until it becomes a part of you.

I was first introduced to this concept by Og Mandino in his book, *The Greatest Salesman in the World* but I have seen hundreds of books now that use some form of this "mind training" to help them rise to better places in their life. In fact, all of us have heard stories of people pinning the thing they desire on a wall or somewhere and looking at it and visualizing it and eventually achieving it. They acquired it because they impressed upon themselves what they desired, and their subconscious embraced it as fact and powerfully moved to make it a reality in their life. What others have done to get objects of desire or higher positions of power or wealth, we will use to graft God's truths into our hearts and minds until new habits of love and acceptance are formed. God created these amazing minds that we have, both conscious and subconscious, and we can use the tools God has given us to grow closer to Him and closer to our purpose. Where your life was marred by negative thoughts constantly, we can retrain the mind to embrace the beauty all around it and the greatness that God has placed within us and we can reach our higher high. So let's create YOUR unique mantra and then as you repeat it morning and night, you will see the change happen from within.

CREATING YOUR MANTRA

Your mantra should be both an affirmation of who you are in Christ and address the areas that you struggle in with new positive affirmations that begin to embrace the new habits of love and acceptance you want to embody. Scripture should be part of it either directly in quotes or in spirit. I believe it should start with bold statements of who you are in Christ and what God says about you! I'm going to share the one I created. Then we can break it down so you can get the concept, and we can work together to form your unique mantra. So let's start.

Brian's Mantra....

"I am a child of God created in His perfect image and indwelled by the perfect Holy Spirit. My body is completely healthy and perfect in form. My mind is linked to the mind of Christ and flows love effortlessly with no fear, for fear does not exist where love flows. The Spirit of God is free to reign in me to heal others and myself. I release all areas of my life to Him. My loved ones, my family, my business, my relationships, and my ministry, I completely release to Him for He can do a better job with my life than I can. I will stay alert to His direction and simply do what He guides me to do. I bring glory to God as I effortlessly do the Father's Will allowing Him to direct my steps. His yoke is easy and His burden is light. My mind, heart and soul is grafted to Christ and all things are given to me as I live this life abundantly as Christ Promised. I bless others out of the overflow of love and success and bring glory to God daily. This is why I, Brian Peart, was created - to glorify God and I now do it daily."

Simple. Just a paragraph. It does not need to be long, but it needs to speak God's truth about WHO you are, and it needs to address the areas of weakness that are holding you back. After writing that down in my journal, I also copied it to a piece of paper and taped it to my mirror in my bathroom. Every morning when I wake up, I read it as part of my morning quiet time. Each night as I brush my teeth before going to bed, I read it again. Slowly, these truths are working into me and creating a new man.

Now let's break the pieces of this mantra down and focus on writing one for you. <u>PLEASE DON'T SKIP THIS STEP</u>. I know, you may say, "Brian, I don't really need to do this. I know all this stuff" or "This seems like something out of a new age book, and I don't want to do this." You may say, "This was easy for you but how do I write something like this?" I tell you, DON'T SKIP THIS STEP.

If you are broken, if you are brokenhearted, and you want to move past it to victory, you MUST begin to control the inner dialogue going on in your head. Yes, this takes some effort but it is worth it. We are talking about changing habits and demons that may have been limiting you for years. **This is vitally important!** And there is nothing new age about writing down what God says about you in Scripture and claiming it as your own. Please work on your own mantra and embrace the daily regimen of reading these truths, and you will see NEW and BETTER habits beginning to form. You will be ready for the final step, planning your higher high. Let's continue with breaking the pieces of this mantra down so we can create your own powerful mantra. We have blank pages at the back of this book that you can use to work on the mantra, or you can use a journal or any notepad. But this is something to write down, to think about, to spend some time working on. This is the beginning of a glorious future, the first step in a great journey. So let's get started.

I believe the mantra should begin with a powerful statement of truth about you in God's eyes, a powerful Scripture verse that resonates with you but talks about who we are in Christ. Most people don't realize how glorious they are, and they NEED to embrace it to really be all they were called to be. Is there some Scripture that relates to you, the truth of your glory, that just has always moved you? IF not, as you read this book, especially Chapter 2, what Scripture verses jumped out at you as truths about you? One that blows me away is that we were made in His image, and He is perfect. Jesus said, "Be thee perfect as my heavenly father is perfect" (Matthew 5:48, KJV). That verse has always challenged me, so I started my mantra with that bold statement.

"I am a child of God created in His perfect image and indwelled by the perfect Holy Spirit."

I need to embrace this truth, deep down, on a cellular level because I have always struggled with insecurity. That's why I wanted my mantra to start off with BOLD

TRUTH about who I am in Christ. I have security in Him, and I need not be insecure ever again. I encourage you to find a similar opening statement that is a bold affirmation of who you are...fearfully and wonderfully made. Make sure it is Scripture based and focused on who you are in Christ, a new creation. Go ahead and write that first bold truth down. Have you done it? Congratulations! Your powerful Mantra has begun! Next, we need to address the areas you struggle with Spiritually or emotionally and reclaim new truths that will become the cornerstone of the future you.

List the two or three areas where you currently struggle in your walk with the Lord or your life, the chains that limit you reaching full effectiveness. They could be things you have struggled with your whole life, or they may be something that you have just come to realize from your time of pain or suffering. Whatever they are, you know what thoughts limit you. There is no one looking. Total honesty is critical here. What things are limiting you from becoming greater in Christ? What things are limiting your life? For me, I listed the following:

- Fear/insecurity

- trying too hard

- not letting go and letting God

Let me break these down so you get the idea.

FEAR/INSECURITY

For me, if I am deeply honest, I am afraid of losing control. I am afraid of being rejected. I am afraid of failing and disappointing people that count on me or look up to me. People who know me would be surprised at this statement. The truth is, in my quiet place where no one sees, I am insecure. For me, fear and insecurity flow together, feeding off each other. My morning quiet time helps combat these feelings, but they still manifest themselves in many ways.

In my marriage, when my ex-wife withdrew her love, it freaked me out. My insecurity and fear drove me to try to "fix" the problem. I tried to get her back to that glorious love we had the first year of our marriage. She was unhappy. She was struggling in many areas, and I HAD to try to fix it. As I went to Scripture daily in my quiet time, I would see verse after verse that to me clearly told her what she needed to do and would tell her that. Day after day, I told her Scripture she needed to follow to fix her problem.

But she was not in a place to accept these truths. She was struggling and did not want to hear it. You, reader, are seeking answers. You are ready for truth, but she was not. How it came across to her was that I was brow beating her with the Word of God, pointing out her failures daily and beating her up with God's Word. I was actually driving her further away. My fears of losing her, of failing in marriage, my deep insecurities were all driving me to find the answer for HER instead of letting her focus on God and figure it out herself. Instead of just listening, trusting God to work in her, and just being a calm supporter, I was driven to "fix" her. This is one of the areas that drove her furthest away, and at its root was my fear and insecurity. So I needed to counter this deep fear with a verse that speaks God's TRUTH into the situation. I chose "perfect love casts out fear" (1 John 4:18). I just rewrote it.

"My mind is linked to the mind of Christ and I flow love effortlessly with NO FEAR for fear does not exist where love flows."

NOT LETTING GO AND LETTING GOD/TRYING TOO HARD

The second area is really an area that God has been hammering on me for years. Is there some area where you just know that you need to work on, that God has pointed out to you over and over? For me, this was it. It seems I am constantly falling short in this area, trying to do too much. Even the above example of my ex-wife shows a man who is trying way too hard to fix everything. When in truth, I KNOW, I mean, I just KNOW that God can do all of this better. I need look no further than my son to see how much better God is at running my life than I am.

My first son, Zachery, was my pride and joy from the moment he was born. He was an easy baby. He was a good-hearted boy. As he got to be older, like eight or nine, he just wanted to be with me all the time. If I had to run up to Home Depot for something, he wanted to go with me. He was my little buddy. It was fatherhood at its best. I really don't even remember him doing much wrong prior to high school. He was just a great kid. But then, between his eighth grade and ninth grade years, he got introduced to marijuana. Now you can say it is a "mellow" drug and not "bad" like the others but for my boy, it caused a change in his attitude. Combined with natural teenage rebellion, it led to a tough four years. This perfect kid who never did anything wrong was lying and arguing and bucking my authority at every turn. I stayed diligent, punishing him time and time again, taking away cars, grounding him, disciplining him constantly, but he kept doing it. He wore me down.

After three and a half years of fighting him, I finally had no other option. I kicked him out of my house. I sent him packing to his mom's and literally washed my hands of him. I would not even talk to him. It was the hardest thing I had ever done and it hurt me horribly, but I knew it was the right thing. I could not stop him from disobeying, from drugs, from rebellion. I literally released him to the Lord. I told God, "God, I have tried everything. I can't get through. I release him to you Lord. PLEASE move in his heart." I prayed daily for him, but I basically cut him off otherwise. **Not even three months later, he came back to me, telling me that he had gotten saved again and wanted me to baptize him again!**

I was SO happy. He had gone to a Wednesday night youth group, and it was like the pastor was speaking right to him. He would ask a question in his mind, and the pastor would be addressing that very thing within a minute or two. It was powerful and it moved him deeply. As I write this, it is almost two years later. He works for me now and is doing great. He starts his day with Bible reading and prayer, then attacks his work. He is constantly talking to his friends about Jesus. He is my pride and joy again. **<u>I WORKED THREE AND A HALF YEARS TO TRY TO GET HIM BACK ON TRACK AND FAILED MISERABLY AND IT TOOK GOD JUST THREE MONTHS!</u>** And it stuck! He is still doing great two years later. It was a powerful lesson to me. ANYTHING I CAN DO, GOD CAN DO BETTER. Not only that, He promises us He WILL.

In Jesus' Sermon on the Mount, He shares the simple truth of living a great life on this planet. "Do not be worried about your life, as to what you will eat or what you will drink, nor for your body as to what you will put on. Is not life more than food and the body more than clothing? Look at the birds in the air, that they do not sow, nor do they reap nor gather into barns, and yet your heavenly Father feeds them. Are you not worth much more than they?" (Matthew 6:25 & 26).

"Be still and KNOW that I am God" (Psalm 46:10).

"My yoke is easy and my burden is light" (Matthew 11:30).

"I have come, that you may have life, and have it abundantly" (John 10:10).

Over and over, Jesus promises that if we will just trust Him, just release to Him all our cares and worries, that He will take care of us. I honestly just cannot believe how amazing that TRUTH is. He really will take care of us. He will take our burdens and help us through. I have seen Him do it over and over and over again in my life. Yet, after seeing Him take care of a problem in a miraculous way, it seems the next problem that comes along, I jump right into fixing it instead of just taking it to the Lord. I was finally over trying to be "Mr. Fix It." I stink at it to be candid. God REALLY is much better. I had to make it a new habit, and habits are formed by repetition, so I added this into my mantra.

"I release all areas of my life to Him. My loved ones, my family, my business, my relationships and my ministry I completely release to Him for He can do a better job with my life than I can. I will stay alert to His direction and simply do what He guides me to do. His yoke is easy and His burden is light."

It is so much simpler to just release to Jesus, but for a person with a lifetime habit of trying too hard and trying to make it all right for everyone, it took forming a new thought pattern in my mind. I then ended my mantra with my hope for the future, what I always wanted to be deep in my heart. I want to be a blessing to others. I want to glorify my King. It is the deep, deep desire of my heart. I ended the mantra with that statement of faith.

"My mind, heart and soul is grafted to Christ and all things are given to me as I live this life abundantly as Christ promised. I bless others out of the overflow of love and success and bring glory to God daily. This is why I, Brian Peart, was created - to glorify God and I now do it daily."

It is really not that hard. The outline is kind of simple:

1. Opening bold statement about who you are in Christ

2. One or two areas of weakness addressed with Scripture that claims God's truth into that weakness

3. Ending statement with a bold statement about your future based on the TRUTH of God's Word.

Now you may be thinking that you cannot find Scriptures that will speak about your weakness because you do not know the Bible that well. That is just an excuse. In this day and age, you have that knowledge at your fingertips with Google search. Do you struggle with pornography? Type in, "Scripture verses to help fight pornography" and then see what comes up. Scroll the different Bible Verses until you find one that speaks directly to you. WORD OF CAUTION: Be sure to grab a Scripture verse. Understand that anyone can post anything on the internet so make sure that you grab a verse that counteracts that problem. If you go to the internet, be careful. Search for Bible Verses that address the problem. When you come to the right one you will know it. It will resonate with you. Add that verse to your mantra.

ONLY address two, at most, three areas of weakness. Keep in mind, many of the little things we struggle with are really just symptoms of the bigger problem. For example, I know a woman who is loved by a great guy. He was faithful, adored her, provided a great life for her, but she cheated on him anyway. She cheated on him with a guy who was half the man that her husband was, and she knew it. She did not want to cheat on him, but she could not seem to help herself. She ultimately ended the marriage with divorce. She also would often pick at her nails until she bled, like crazy picking at them, sometimes ripping the whole nail off. Now these may seem like two different issues but they really stem from the same cause. Deep down in her subconscious, she does not feel lovely. She does not feel worthy of being loved by a Godly man. When faced with a love of a good man, she sabotaged that love because she did not feel she was worthy. By the form of self-mutilation she was doing to her nails, she was outwardly attempting to make herself less attractive, more in line with the way she really views herself on the inside. Now much of this stems from some childhood trauma, things that were not her fault. But here she is, still dealing with them in her 40's. AND THIS IS NOT UNCOMMON. Many of us deal with issues from our childhood our whole lives. But in the end, there are not two problems here, there is one. She does not embrace what God says about her. She does not truly believe, deep down, that she is worthy of love and happiness. She could type into Google, "Bible verses that deal with self-loathing" and as she reads through, find the one that resonates with her. Make sure yours resonates with you and it is Scripture. "All Scripture is inspired by God and profitable for teaching, for reproof, for correction, for training in righteousness so that the man of God may be adequate, equipped for every good work" (2 Timothy 3:16 & 17).

So choose just one or two issues to deal with and then find the verse that counters that problem. My fear and insecurity I listed as one because they really feed off each other and are just one big problem. So keep this simple. You know what the heart of the matter is. Deep down, you know what your biggest problem is. Look at your life, take your time and look at the consistent issues you struggle with and condense them to the big one or two issues that have held you back your whole life. Then find a Bible verse that counters them. Add it to your mantra and through the power of daily repetition, you can retrain your

mind to think differently about this problem. GOD HAS
GIVEN US THESE AMAZING MINDS THAT WE CAN
EITHER USE FOR GOOD OR MISUSE FOR BAD. Let's
start using them for good. Start with a powerful opening
statement about the truth of who you are in Christ. Address
the one or two big spiritual problems in your life that have
been holding you back with Scripture that speaks truth
into that situation. And then finally, end with a powerful
statement of your bold future.

So what does that look like? What is the statement
of your bold future? You see what I put, to glorify God
daily. And in many ways, as Christians, that really is
the purpose of all of us. For me, bringing glory to God
daily means something very specific. It means being an
example in everything I do and allowing God to get all the
credit and all the glory. For me, someone who has always
craved attention and affirmation, giving God all the glory
is actually NOT easy. It is actually something I need to
stay focused on, something I get challenged on daily as
a stressed-out client may bite my head off. I need to still
glorify the Lord. It is hard sometimes. It is something that
I need to work on, and that I need to speak truth into and
is Scripture based. It is also big enough to encompass the
future that God has planned for me. For me, this is the
best way to end my mantra. This is the bold statement. It
works for me. You may feel you have a different purpose.
You may have a different calling. What I ended my mantra
with may not resonate with you at all. And that is good!

This is YOUR mantra, YOUR life. There is no right answer to this process. You, and only you, need to go to God and determine what you are put on this earth for and what your purpose is. IF you are not sure, then we need to work on this until you find that bold statement of your future "you" to end this mantra with. This is going to be, in a sense, your mission statement. In Chapter 4 we will go over planning your future but it is going to key off of this vision you cast right here. DON'T SKIP THIS STEP! THIS IS ONE OF THE MOST IMPORTANT THINGS YOU WILL EVER DO. Essentially, we are working on the eternal question of all mankind.

"Why am I here?" What is my future? What is my purpose? Obviously, this is going to be the key to your future, so it is worth spending some time getting this right. AND THANKFULLY, GOD DOES NOT LEAVE US ALONE TO FIGURE THIS OUT ON OUR OWN. When you were a child, you had no problem knowing what your parents wanted you to do. They clearly told you. God is also very clear on certain things in His Word, and we need not guess on what God calls us to do. Some very clear commands of Scripture are a great starting point to figuring out your purpose. Of course, the granddaddy of commands for the Christian is the Great Commandment.

"You shall love the Lord your God with all your heart, and with all your soul, and with all your mind. This is the great and foremost commandment. The second is like it, you shall love your neighbor as yourself" (Matthew 22:37-39).

We have to get this piece right. The more I go through life, the more I realize that putting God first, loving Him above myself or family, leads to a better life for me AND my family. Love God. Love others. It seems simple, but your ending vision does not have to be complicated. It needs to be bold. It needs to be in sync with God and what He says in His Word and broad enough to encompass a wonderful future, but it can be simple.

Another critical passage is the Great Commission.

"Go therefore and make disciples of all nations, baptizing them in the name of the Father and of the Son and of the Holy Spirit, teaching them to observe all that I commanded you and lo, I am with you always, even to the end of the age." (Matthew 28:19 & 20)

I have seen many churches condense this into a mission statement, "To know Him and make Him known." Which I like a lot. Simple but puts the main thing as the main thing. What is that main thing? Jesus. Rick Warren, in his best seller, "Purpose Driven Life" stated it beautifully in the opening chapter. "It's not about you...it's about God."[6] It's about God. Your big picture vision MUST include God if you are going to truly live a fulfilled life. God is the

---

6   Rick Warren, *The Purpose Driven Life* (Ohio: Zondervan, 2006).

heart of the matter. "For from Him and through Him and to Him are all things. To Him be the glory forever, Amen" (Romans 11:36).

So how does this all manifest for you and specifically for your big picture vision for the future? You may feel that these statements are too broad for you, but not necessarily. Do you struggle in any of these areas? Do you struggle to put God first? Do you spend most of your time worrying about your job or your kids, or are you truly focusing on God first? If we fail at the main thing, everything else will feel out of sync. If you are not nailing the Great Commission and the Great Commandment, you probably need to work them into your bold statement of your future. At the very least, your bold vision MUST be in line with the Great Commission and Great Commandment. It must be in sync. For me, to glorify God in all that I do encompasses both of these statements, as it is impossible to glorify God without embodying His core principles. For me, that really is the heart of the matter.

Be careful not to confuse roles with broad vision. You may feel led to be a missionary, or a pastor, or a business man or a great parent. Those are all important roles, but they are not broad enough to encompass your purpose. The missionary has a purpose - to reach the lost. The mother has a purpose - to raise Godly kids. Your purpose, what you choose to make it, needs to focus on God. Specifically, embodying some form of the Great Commandment and the Great Commission. As long as you do that, you are going to be OK. Take some time and try to wrap up this mantra with your bold purpose or vision. If you are still struggling some with it, do the best you can. As we go through the next chapter and plan your future, you will get a better feel for how this all plays together. By the time we are done, you will have a great mantra that will truly capture the essence of who you are in Christ and where you are going!

Congratulations! You have achieved so much already. If you have been working as we go along, then you have prayed for forgiveness and put away the past. You have created a new mantra that embraces the truth of who you are, addresses your key areas of weakness and sets out a bold future for you. This mantra, with constant repetition, will become a part of you forming the new habits and the new man or woman that you had always hoped to be. At first, as you repeat the mantra, you will not realize that it is even working but soon the transformation will be evident to all around you. You have done so much already, but we are not done yet. Now, we need to craft a battle plan for your future. Your glorious future is right around the corner!

My Thoughts on Chapter 3:

Chapter 4:

God's Perfect Plan for Your Future

"For I know the plans I have for you says the Lord, plans to prosper you, not to harm you - to give you a future and a hope" (Jeremiah 29:11).

Adrian Rogers, in his book, *The Wonder of It All*, shared the following about this passage and I think it is worth repeating.

"I can tell you, on the authority of the Word of God, that He has a wonderful plan for you. Some find that hard to believe because they're afraid if they let go of their agenda, God may send them off to a remote jungle or call them to a life of singleness. Friend, God's plan will be the best thing that has ever happened to you! His thoughts are higher than our thoughts."[7]

---

7   Ibid., 20.

He knows what is best for us. This can seem like a daunting task, planning your future. You read the above verse and you say, "Yes Brian, God knows the plans He has for me, but how do I figure it out?" That is what we will tackle in this chapter. Although we are not God, we have a vision for our lives now that focuses on Him. And God is VERY clear in Scripture that we have a RESPONSIBILITY TO PLAN OUR LIVES. Proverbs 16:9 says, "The mind of man plans his way but the Lord directs the steps."

We have a responsibility to plan our way and we are also to let God direct the steps. That subtle balance is the key to great planning for the Godly man or woman. Until I really got this verse, I was guilty of planning the steps. Lots of to do's in all the areas of my life. As a father, I will do this, this and this. In the role of husband, I will do this, this and this. This is actually micromanaging and counterproductive according to this verse in Proverbs. In fact, most people are guilty of allowing a ton of little things into their weeks, so much so that the Holy Spirit has very little time to lead. ABC lists and to-do lists keep us so focused on the little things we miss all the areas God wants us to really flourish. This is one of Satan's favorite tactics - to keep Christians so busy with little things that do not matter that they bear no meaningful fruit for the kingdom.

Instead of to do lists and task-oriented micro-management, we should plan the few big picture items into our lives and let GOD handle the day to day steps.

Jesus modeled this for us in His own life. He never ran on ahead. He knew the big picture of why He was here, what He needed to do, and He just went about each day doing the task God put in front of Him. Walking from one town to another and meeting a woman at the well, He stops and does what God wanted Him to do. Then on to the next town, to the next step. He taught us in His Sermon on the Mount to just worry about today, and He modeled it for us. Be clear on your big picture. Move in the direction of the plan God has for you and do what He tells you each day. Step by step, God WILL lead you. Soon you will be amazed as you watch Him move in and through you, to change your immediate world and possibly even, a much broader reach than you ever imagined. He has the WHOLE universe at His disposal! He can move in someone you do not even know to give you the encouragement you need at just the right time. There is no way we can do this better than Him. He knows the plans He has for you. If you allow Him to direct the steps, you just may be amazed at how grand that plan is.

I'm going to start with how I did it and share some strategies that will help you get there. As I share my own story, you will begin to get the feel for this and then we can work on YOUR battle plan with a few specific strategies to draw out the two or three areas that God has in mind for you. Soon we can have you focused on the few things that really matter while God moves directly in the steps to bring about His will. It is POWERFUL to live this way, as you will see as I share my story. So, let's begin with that.

My divorce had finalized; I had turned 50, and I was probably having the closest thing to a midlife crisis that you can have. I'm not sure if I had a midlife crisis in the classic sense or whether a crisis just happened to be thrust on me at the midpoint of my life. Either way, I needed direction. I had been a millionaire and lost it. I had started a ministry that had helped thousands and led about 100 people to the Lord, and I was barely involved in it anymore. I had six kids and a business that touched the lives of thousands but here I was…shaken...uncertain...unclear about the next 30 years. Divorce can do that to you. I decided to take a few weeks off, what I called a hiatus, and get alone with God to get clarity on what He wanted from me for the next 30 years. IF you have the means to get a week away to work on this, I highly recommend it. If not, just get some quiet time alone. It is critical to not be distracted by life when you are working on something so critical as your life! Psalm 46:10 tells us to "Be still and know that He is God." We need to get alone, get still and let Him work in us. There in the hotel room with a notepad and a Bible, I began by taking stock of where I was now, knowing that I needed to be faithful where God had placed me. I took out my note pad and began to just write down the roles that God had me in currently.

God had given me six kids. They were a blessing, and a responsibility. I was no longer married, so I was no longer a husband. I had a business with hundreds of clients and literally thousands of people in my sphere of influence. My business, my relationships, my family were all responsibilities. God had placed me in these areas, and it was up to me to flourish in them. Business man, father, family member, church member. These were the areas where I was placed. God wants you to be fruitful there. You do NOT need to look far away. God is working all around you and He wants you to join Him.

As I began to look at those areas, an overwhelming conviction was laid on my heart. I did not do a good job developing these relationships. I had been convicted on this randomly over the years but never really did much about it. In one of my first counseling sessions with Dottie, she asked me about my business. I told her how I made "X" number of calls and really focused on getting the sale and then getting to the next client. She hit me right between the eyes in that annoying sweet way when she said, "Well Brian, do you think Jesus would rush off the phone with every person?" Ugh! No, Jesus would stop and ask the question the people needed to hear. He was never in a rush. I had my excuses as to why I did it. It was the way I always did it.

I even used excuses of giftedness. I would say to myself, "God made me able to be very focused." Oh, I had all my excuses! But the truth is, I had often been convicted of how little I paid attention to the other person on the phone. I was always so busy. I was rushing them off to get to the next thing. I knew the first area I needed to focus on was to be more relational in all my relationships, including at work, at home, with my family and sphere of influence. This became the first "Prong" of my Battle Plan - to be more relational in my entire sphere of influence. Doing so would make me a better dad, leader, and businessman.

I have been labeling this game plan a "Battle Plan" and that is truly what it is. This is your plan to battle the forces that are against you, including, but not limited to, yourself, your relationships, your job, your habits and even the devil himself. We are going to combat that by keeping it simple. A few key strategies are all we are after. They need to be in sync with your big vision and should flow effortlessly from them. In the best battle plans, you never just have one mode of attack. You need to have multiple prongs to your attack. The same is true of your life's battle plan. You need two to three prongs of attack - a few areas that are the big picture things that God Himself has called you to flourish in. My first prong was "Be More Relational in My Sphere of influence." Our prongs should resonate with Scripture. God will NEVER tell you to do something that violates His Word. This certainly matches up with Scripture. God calls us to work in our relationships, to lead them to Him, to encourage them, to love them, and "love your neighbor as yourself" (Mark 12:31). So my first prong matched up with Scripture, but it also supported my big picture goal of glorifying God. Let me explain.

When I stay so busy and focused on me and my tasks, I am not glorifying God in any way. Everything actually is all about me. But when I take two extra seconds and ask that client, "How are things with you?" I am opening myself up to opportunities - to God moving in the discussion and possibly giving me a chance to join Him in changing a life. Now for some of you, this is natural for you and you wonder how I could struggle in this area, but it is just not a habit for me. When I stop watching tv and actually take the time to pray with my child, I am modeling Jesus who took the time to pray with His disciples. Modeling Jesus glorifies God. So, the first prong for me met all the criteria. It was Scriptural. It was in sync with my big picture vision of glorifying God and it allowed me to flourish right where I was, in the people God ALREADY had all around me. I was very excited.

Next, I looked at areas where God had given me specific gifts. Strengths, things I did better than average because God had gifted me in those areas. You see, you were created with certain strengths. God wired you to have strengths in certain areas, and He expects you to use those gifts he has given you to His glory. For me, God had given me strengths in teaching. He gave me an incredible amount of energy which is a blessing, and He has given me the ability to write. I can write tons of copy very easily. I used this in my business to market by writing tips and e-mailing them out consistently, but I had not written a book in years. I did write a book 10 years ago, but it only sold a few thousand copies, and most of those were by my direct selling. So, I kind of shelved this ability as I focused on the urgent - paying the bills. But I knew this was a gift of God, and He wants me to use His gifts for His glory. It became clear then what my second Prong would be - to write another book. This too, met all the main criteria. It was using the gifts God had given me and by writing about my walk with the Lord, I was also glorifying Him. I truly feel that God is writing this book by guiding me into the flow and chapters and content. I am excited to see how it turns out. But there in that hotel in Key Largo, it was becoming clear. God was not done with me yet. In fact, my next 30 years could be VERY exciting, maybe even far more fruitful than I have been up to now. And it is possible just those two prongs would have been fine. That is plenty to add to an already busy plate. But something else had been pressing on me over the last few years...ministry.

God has given me a heart to fund ministry and to be involved in ministry. I first realized this back in 2000 when God laid on my heart to start a ministry to teach Biblical Principles on stewardship to the local churches. As I became obedient to that calling, the ministry Biblical Principles, Inc was begun with my friend and mentor, Bill Prince. God moved in amazing ways in that ministry, serving and teaching and touching thousands. But when Lehman Brothers went down in 2008, that all changed. My business is commercial mortgage brokering - not residential, but commercial. When Lehman Brothers was allowed to fail, what few of us realized was that they were the main buyers of commercial mortgage backed securities. Within three weeks of their bankruptcy, the commercial mortgage market screeched to a halt. We lost 95% of our business in three weeks! The country went through a recession, but my industry went through a full-scale crash. It was a great depression in commercial lending.

Immediately, ministry took a back burner to survival and feeding my family. It took me years to get back to the profitability I had back in 2007. It was long. It was arduous, but finally, I got back to break even. And now that the income was sufficient to meet my basic needs, the pinging on my heart to do ministry was resurfacing again. Don't ignore the prompting of the Holy Spirit. IF GOD IS CONSTANTLY LAYING SOMETHING ON YOUR HEART, THERE IS A REASON. HE WANTS YOU TO DO SOMETHING ABOUT IT!

For me, that was to get involved in local ministry again. What ministry I did not know, and I did not want to pigeon hole God, I just wanted to be open to funding and working with ministries again. It was heavy on my heart, and I wanted to obey the Holy Spirit's prompting. And once again, this prong matched up with Scripture and was in sync with bringing Glory to God, which was my big picture vision. Jesus told us to serve others, to help those who were less fortunate. "Truly I tell you, whatever you did for one of the least of these brothers and sisters of mine, you did for me" (Matthew 25:40, NIV). He gave us the parable of the Good Samaritan to teach us how to love our neighbor. James warns us to make sure our Faith and our Works are in line with each other. There you have it - the sum of hours of thought and strategy - what I called my "3-Pronged Attack" for the next 30 years.

1. Be more relational in my work, home, family and sphere of influence

2. Write another book

3. Get involved in ministry again with my time and talents

Note, these are not specific to-do's. I am not deciding what ministry to serve. I am not setting a goal like "I will be relational with three people today." I am not saying what kind of book I am going to write. I am just laying out three areas of focus that I was going to allow God to work in and leaving the details to Him. I was planning my way but allowing the Lord to direct the steps. Once you see how God directed my steps, how he worked in them and interconnected them, I think you will be excited to get your own two or three-pronged attack going.

PUTTING IT IN PRACTICE

I immediately began to execute these prongs even while still being on my hiatus. I was alone. It was a perfect opportunity to begin writing, so I started this book. Now the exact shape of this book was not fully laid out, but I knew that what I had just gone through, the amazing pain of that divorce, was pressing on my mind. The journey I was on was one that God could use for others if I was bold enough to open up on all the pain and failure. So, I just started writing. I probably got the first few pages done before getting back from my hiatus. At that point, the writing had to be worked into my days, and so I worked on it some mornings and on weekends when I did not have the kids. But the fun was just beginning. As I got back from my hiatus, God immediately began to work in these prongs in amazing ways and also continued to affirm that I was on the right track. One of my first calls was to Bill Prince, and we met up for lunch. At that lunch, I shared these three prongs to which he shared two amazing things.

He had made a partnership with a Christian publishing company, and we were now able to self-publish our own work as long as it was Christian based. Just like that, God paved the way for me to get this book published. Then he shared that my first book, which was over 10 years old and in my mind, a failure because of how few sales it had, had just been used by a pastor to revive his church. It seems the eight deacons were all fighting and the church was getting ready to split when the pastor read my book which was given to him freely by Bill. After reading it, he ordered eight copies and met with the deacons telling them each to read the book and come back in a week to meet and discuss. When they met back again, God had moved in their lives and they opened up and came together. It was almost a revival. These leaders went back in and the church, now with the leadership on the same page, not only did not splinter but began to grow. Now it has already over 1000 people and growing. To me, this was affirmation that I needed to write. But that was just the beginning.

What blew me away was the way God just effortlessly put it all together. It began with my calls. I began to start asking people how they were doing. It led to opportunities to pray for people, even during my business day. And it led to ministry opportunities. One of the relationships I called on was an insurance agent who had referred me to an accountant months before. This accountant was very involved in his client's businesses and was a great source for me, but he never returned my calls so I put the lead aside. But because I took the time to talk with this insurance agent about our businesses, he reminded me that I should call this guy. He gave me his number again and this time, the accountant set up a lunch meeting. That lunch meeting led to him inviting me to the Rotary Club. I had heard of the Rotary Club but I really did not know much about it. Turns out, it is basically successful business men and women who come together to find out about local ministries and serve the local community with their time and money. Basically, exactly what my third prong was. It came about from a meeting with an accountant where instead of talking about just business, we opened up on life.

I joined the club and the second week, a local church leader was talking about the problem with teen drugs and depression. I felt led to stand up and share my own story of my son Zachery which ministered to multiple people there who were going through their own similar struggle with their teens. It also led to lunch with that church leader who introduced me to two local ministries.

Again, none of this was specifically planned, but as each door opened up, because it was in line with my three prongs, I just said yes and stepped through that door. God was directing each step. I was just taking the steps He laid out. Both local ministries were able to use me, and a third ministry was introduced to me by another friend, Philip. My relationship with him had grown from my Wednesday night networking meetings, and we had spent two hours one night talking about the Lord. The head of this third ministry has become one of my dearest friends and supporters. Just like that, I was on the board of two new ministries. The relationship with Philip had ramifications on my writing as he invited me to speak on his radio program. Sitting in the waiting room at the station, I saw a book on the coffee table by Adrian Rogers - the one I have quoted twice in this book. There was dust on the book, as most people who went there did not know who he was, but he was one of Bill's favorite preachers. As I started thumbing through the small book, God clearly showed me the basis of the first two chapters of this book. I asked the girl if I could keep the book and she said, "Sure, no one has looked at that in a year." The outline for my book was coming into shape and in fact, God was basically laying it all out for me while I was waiting to be interviewed on the radio about my business! He just kept moving in every area and building into every other area in ways I could not have possibly planned.

In a little over three months after coming back from the hiatus, I now was on the board of two new ministries, was finished writing my new book, had a host of new friends and relationships and was growing all my relationships in new and powerful ways. I did it while keeping my business going. In fact, God was blessing my business as well. As I finish writing this, my business is the strongest it has been since the early 2000's. My relationships with my family and kids was growing and I was using the same 24 hours I had before. If I would have set goals and doubled my efforts, there is no way I would have a book completed, be put on the board of two new ministries and have no less than 10 excellent new friends that I communicate with constantly all while growing my business to new heights of profitability. My relationship with my employee, Mary, has grown to a true loving bond as she shares her walk and struggles daily with me. It is all so amazing and it all was done by simply doing the next thing God put in front of me. No stress, no worry, just keeping focused in three areas and doing the next step as God directs. I am telling you this is amazing. God has the whole universe at His disposal to move the pieces of your life. You just have to trust Him with the steps. And as I look at Scripture, we see no other authority then Jesus Himself using this same technique.

Yes, Jesus came to pay the price for our sins. That was His big picture vision and purpose for being here, but he accomplished it by focusing on a few prongs which He proclaimed in Luke 4:18. "The Spirit of the Lord is upon me, because He has anointed me to preach the gospel to the poor, he has sent me to proclaim release to the captives, and recovery of sight to the blind, to set free those who are oppressed." If you read the Gospel accounts of Jesus' life, this is exactly what He did. Every day He got up, prayed, and walked out to preach the gospel, heal the sick and set people free. He had a big vision (the Cross) but He just focused on the few big things He was gifted and called to do and then each day just did those things to whoever was put in front of Him. We never see Him rush. He was never in a hurry but always on time, and we can follow His lead. We can focus the big picture of our life on Him, begin to move in the main areas that are uniquely given to us, and then just do the next step God gives you as each day unfolds. It is exciting to wake up and know that God may just be up to something big that day and all you need to do is just obey. He says His yoke is easy and His burden is light. By letting Him direct the steps, the entire universe is at His disposal to bring things into your life that you could never imagine. All you have to worry about is the few things YOU have already been gifted or blessed with. So let's go ahead and work on YOUR big picture battle plan. It begins by starting where you are.

YOUR BATTLE PLAN

We are prompted to bear fruit right where we are. It is important to understand exactly where God has placed us. The roles we discussed earlier are definitely part of the field that God has placed you in. As we begin this process, I ask you to stop right now and pray. Ask God to come into this time and give you wisdom. Ask Him to protect you during this time and not allow Satan to have any room in this time. Pray His power and wisdom on this time. Then grab a piece of paper or use the sheets at the back of this book, and let's get started laying out the roles that God has you in right now.

IF you are married, that is definitely one area that you are called to be fruitful in. That husband or wife was given ONE partner – YOU – and it is your job to bear fruit. Now you may say, "Brian, you don't understand, he is this or that" or "Brian, we have not been in sync in years and there is no chance of fixing it." I tell you that you do not realize the power of the God you serve. "With God all things are possible" (Matthew 19:26). Jesus Himself claimed it. If you have a red-letter bible that puts Jesus' words in red, this statement would be red letter. The Lord Himself says ALL things are possible, so let Him figure it out. If you are married, then this is likely one prong you need to list. Your marriage affects your life, your kids, and your future. If you don't know how you can possibly fix the marriage, THAT IS OK. You are not going to figure out the steps. You just claim it as an area that you will work toward God's glory and let HIM direct your steps. You don't have to figure this out. You just have to acknowledge a willingness to focus on this area and let God lead. If you can get your spouse to do this as well, then I tell you a glorious marriage is VERY possible. If not, it doesn't matter. You have a responsibility to do your best with your part. If that person does not reciprocate, it does not matter. You just keep obeying God and trust. I am passionate about marriage. My heart breaks that I am divorced. I am embarrassed about it, but my wives committed adultery and in the end, left me. Even then, I tried to convince them to come back but in both situations, they chose not to. I am absolutely sure that had they committed to the marriage, God would have worked in it and healed the marriage, even with adultery. I know one marriage where the husband cheated on the wife with no less than 20 women and yet they have put it back together. If God could move there, He can fix your situation. How? Don't worry about it. LET HIM DIRECT THE STEPS. You just list it as one of your prongs.

If you have kids, then that too is a ministry that God has given you. Those kids were given one mom, one dad. You need to pour into them as best you can. How? Let God direct you. As I thought through where God had placed me, He has given me six kids. I provide for them and give them unconditional love, but I knew I could do better. I could improve my relationship with them. As you list these roles, look for common recurring themes. For me, relationship was a recurring theme. By having relationships as my first prong, I was addressing this area with my kids as well. God just leads and I follow. I took my sons with me on a business trip, prompted by God in this relationship area. I am going to a concert with my daughter, again, something God worked out. The tickets were given to me, and then the person who gave them to me backed out, which opened the door to go to the concert with my oldest daughter who shares the same love for music that I do. I didn't plan it, God worked out the step.

IMPORTANT. Once you settle on a prong, make sure it matches up with Scripture and matches up with your big picture vision. God is passionate for marriage, He hates divorce (Malachi 2:16). He is a good father and cares about the children. Growth in these areas definitely meshes with Scripture. Make sure it matches with your big picture vision, whatever that is. IF it matches with both of these areas and is something that you need to improve and work on, then it is likely a great prong for you. You just list the prong, the big focus, and don't worry about the little steps. God will handle that how He sees fit, and He will do a better job of it than you will. Just trust Him.

Other areas you have been placed is your current work place. You may hate your job, but God calls you to bear fruit right there. If you are self-employed, you have many opportunities to see God work. I have probably learned more about God through my business than any other area. Self-employment can be tough. What an opportunity! Maybe you are currently involved in a ministry and you want to grow that, or you are involved in church and you want to grow there. List all the areas you are currently in roles and look for the area of greatest need or the consistent theme throughout these areas. You are in those areas for a purpose. No one else can fill the role you are currently in. You need to blossom there. Take the time to think through these roles where you have been placed and think of the one thing that God is laying on your heart in these areas. Maybe one area is dominating your thoughts and mind, like your marriage. Your prong could be something like this…

I will honor God in my marriage.

How? Doesn't matter. God will figure that out if you trust Him. He directs the steps! This is easier than you think! You just put the commitment down to honoring God in your marriage. Then, make that a prong. Maybe you are struggling with your teen. Hey, that can be a prong.

I will model Christ for my kids so they will learn to glorify God.

How? Don't worry about that right now. You just need to commit to the big picture desire and let God direct the steps. "But Brian, I need to have a three-part plan for raising my kids." No you don't. You need to let go and let God. You need to turn them over to Him and let Him guide you on the next step with that child. Jesus modeled it. I have applied it. This works! Anything you can do, God can do better! Let me repeat that. ANYTHING YOU CAN DO, GOD CAN DO BETTER! Let Him work THROUGH you to touch that marriage, that child, that co-worker. It is likely your efforts are actually short circuiting what God wants to do, so stop! Stop the micromanaging and trust a God who is far more powerful than you can ever imagine.

Do you get it? Take the time to think of what God wants you to do in these roles. BUT DON'T GO CRAZY. The most you should have is three prongs and we have not gotten to the areas of your giftedness. If you have one prong in the areas God has already placed you, and one prong in the area of your giftedness, that is probably plenty. Remember, as you grow these prongs may change. It is also possible that God intends for you to use your giftedness IN one or more of these roles you are in. So let's talk about the next big consideration - your gifts.

All of us have areas of strengths that are actually blessings from God. Maybe you have the gift of empathy. You can feel the hurt when you are speaking to someone. What a BLESSED GIFT. I wish I had that. I just don't. If I have not specifically experienced something, I have trouble feeling that person's pain, but those with empathy can feel that pain, relate and touch the person in a way that glorifies God. What a gift. Maybe God wants you to focus that gift in one or more of your roles. Take a piece of paper or use the worksheets in the back of this book and start writing down all the areas that God has gifted you in. For me, writing was something. Maybe you are good at public speaking, or maybe you have an athletic ability, or a particular wisdom or skill. Maybe you have raised exceptional kids and you have specific things you do in that area that led to your success. Wow, what a thing that would be to share with others.

Maybe you have the gift of prayer. Some people are prayer warriors. They have the gift of powerful intercessory prayer. WOW, what a God honoring gift. Use that gift. Maybe you are great at keeping in touch with people. Don't minimize your skills or gifts. My brother is great at keeping in touch with people, and he uses it to minister to people whether he realizes it or not. When I was going through the divorce, he called me constantly just to check on me. He was not calling to minister. He did not preach. We just talked. Such a simple thing, but it really helped. People need to be touched by people who care. Maybe you are that caring type of person. USE IT. The world NEEDS your gifts.

Maybe God has given you the ability to teach. What a thing to harness for the kingdom. Maybe He has given you the gift of musical ability. Wow, what a way to minister to people. I know music has played a big part in my life. Bands like 10th Avenue North or Chris Tomlin have been a big blessing in my life. Well hey, they are just using their giftedness. The music team at my church is a blessing. They are just using their giftedness. ANYTHING you are good at can be a ministry opportunity. It could be an area where God will help others. We all have our parts to play. Yes, the athlete like Tim Tebow has a big platform but you have your part to play.

Maybe you have the amazing ability to forgive people easily and show grace. Wow, what a gift. Maybe God wants you to be that forgiving person in your children's lives, and your work life, and your marriage. Maybe you only change your spouse and your three children, but that can impact generations. It is huge! Jesus changed the world through just 12 people. Tim Tebow has his role. You have yours. As long as you are both equally faithful to your roles, you will both be rewarded similarly in Heaven. Jesus shares as much in the Parable of the Talents. WOW.

Whatever area you are strong in, put it as a prong. Use the talent God gave you. The only sin, is not using your talent. In the Parable of the Talents, the person who buried their talents caught the wrath of the master. Maybe you are great at witnessing. Some people are better at that then others. We are all called to bear witness but some people just excel at it. Some people just have an ability of taking any situation and showing how God is at work. What an area to use. Maybe people tell you all the time that you are so good at this or that. List it!

Hopefully you are getting the idea. Maybe you have multiple gifts. Ask God where He wants you to focus. Pray about it. Then list it as a prong:

"I will use my gift of _____ to glorify the Lord."

How? Doesn't matter. You don't need to figure that out right now. God will direct you each day and bring the opportunities each day for you to bear fruit. He is likely doing that right now anyway. You are just not focusing on it. By listing it as a prong, you begin the process of focusing on where God is working. We notice what we focus on. Have you ever bought a car? Maybe you bought a new Honda Accord. That first week you have the car, you are blown away at how many people have Honda Accords. You are taking the same roads you took last week but now you notice all these Hondas on the road. Why? Because you are taking notice. That same principle applies here.

By listing the area of giftedness as something you will begin to pay attention to, God will bring you opportunities constantly to bear fruit. Wait till you see this happen, it will blow you away. You can bear SO much more fruit, right now, right where you are and you will NOT be working any harder. In fact, it will be easier. It will just flow because God is partnering with you. What a blessing.

Don't be discouraged if you start realizing all the opportunities you have already missed, or the mistakes you have already made. YOU CAN NOT CHANGE THE PAST. This is not about who you were. This is about who you are now and who you will become as God works in and through you. Yes, we have made many mistakes. As I was listing down my strengths and roles, I often cried. The divorce was still fresh and the feeling of failure was very prevalent. As you start realizing how powerful God is and yet you still failed, you may want to beat yourself up. DON'T. We will talk in the next chapter about the tricks that Satan uses to keep you down, and this is one of them. You are NOT your past. You are a NEW creation. Keep working on your roles and your gifts and jot them all down. As you do, be aware of the Holy Spirit's prompting. Especially pay attention if you have a particular burden or a particular prompting.

I had a burden for ministry, so I added that as a prong. Maybe your heart is just burdened for your children. If you have a heavy burden, it is likely that is an area that needs to be focused on. Make it a prong. Or maybe you have just been convicted for years in a certain area, list it down. No one is watching. This is YOUR list. You don't have to share it. Maybe you have a particular area of weakness or sin you have struggled with for years, write it down as a prong. If you have a particular conviction, that is none other than the Holy Spirit of God prompting you. Obey that prompting. Maybe you have struggled with pornography for years and you can't seem to overcome it. When no one is looking, it rears its ugly head and you constantly find yourself on your knees apologizing to God for your weakness in that area. Then it is likely this should be a prong:

"I will conquer the demon of pornography once and for all."

How? Don't worry about that right now. God will begin to bring you the people, the books, the teachers, the tools you need to conquer this demon. You just have to be aware when He is prompting you and do exactly what He says. God can conquer this demon. All of this is under His authority. He has power over all darkness and He gives US THAT POWER through the name of Jesus. "But Brian, you don't understand. I have struggled with this sin all my life." So what? Ordinary people can do amazing things through the power of Jesus Christ. In Acts 3 is one of the most encouraging stories that illustrates the power we have in the name of Jesus. It involves Peter, the same disciple that denied God three times. I love Peter because he is so bold but also so flawed. He was just a man, a passionate man, but a flawed man, just like you and me. Peter and John were heading up to the temple to pray when they came across a lame man. Let's pick up the story there...

"And a man who had been lame from his mother's womb was being carried along, whom they used to set down every day at the gate of the temple which is called Beautiful, in order to beg alms of those who were entering the temple. When he saw Peter and John about to go into the temple he begged asking to receive alms. But Peter, along with John, fixed his gaze on him and said, 'look at us!' And he began to give them his attention expecting to receive something from them. But Peter said, 'I do not possess silver and gold, but what I do have I give to you, in the name of Jesus Christ the Nazarene-Walk!' And seizing him by the right hand, he raised him up and immediately his feet and his ankles were strengthened. With a leap he stood upright and began to walk; and he entered the temple with them walking and leaping and praising God" (Acts 3:2-8).

This man was unable to walk since birth. Maybe you have been wrapped in this sin for 20 years. What is that to God? Nothing. If Peter, a flawed man, could make a lame person walk with the power of Jesus's name, you can conquer this demon in the same powerful name. The name of Jesus has the same power as it did then. We just don't have the same burning faith. So claim victory over this conviction, this sin, this thing that has laid heavy on your heart for years. Don't worry about the how, just list it as an area that the Lord will work in and leave the steps to God. He will bring the support people into your life. He will bring what you need to overcome this. He will bring the strength. He will bring the opportunities. He will bring that song that addresses the situation just at the moment of weakness. He will bring you everything you need just at the right moment, things you cannot possibly script or plan. As you obey His simple daily steps, you will become more and more free. And soon, He will bring you others that YOU can mentor and help through the process. He will use you to free others. What a blessing! God can turn this area that you have struggled your whole life into the heart of your future ministry. He can use your struggle to change the world! He just needs you to claim the victory and then obey in the daily steps.

Keep working on this until you have your two to three prongs. Once you do, you are ready to put it all into action...it's go time!

PUTTING IT ALL INTO ACTION

So here we are. It's go time. You have your mantra written down. You have your two or three prongs that will be your future you going forward. Now it's time to put it all together and put it into action. The first step is to get the mantra written down and placed wherever you will see it to read it each morning and each night. For me, I do my quiet time in the morning and I have it written in my journal. That page is marked and reading my mantra is just part of my morning quiet time. Then I have it taped to the mirror in my bathroom where I can read it again at night while I brush my teeth. Maybe you keep it on your nightstand. The key is making it EASY to read, morning and night. Begin to read this mantra each morning and each night. Day by day, as you do this, the Lord will be working to bring it about. You are claiming HIS promises. You are addressing life-long problems with new positive statements. You are casting your big vision for the future. Day by day, you will be getting more positive. You will be growing. You will feel stronger, more confident. It may not seem like anything is happening at first but it won't take long. Soon, people will be telling you, "There is something different about you." It will become evident. Relationships will improve. Everything will improve. So, the first step is the daily reading of that mantra. Every day, morning and night.

Although it takes only 21-30 days, you will probably want to continue to do the reading after those 21 days. I am. I still do it morning and night. It is a good habit now. Also, over time, you may tweak the mantra to address new areas as you get victory over the previous struggles. That is OK. Just go back to Chapter 3 of this book and use the same steps to tweak your mantra. What happens if you skip a weekend? Start over. Just stay consistent. We will discuss slipping up in the next chapter...but for now, just start again. Failure is never final unless you give up. Just start back the next day with your mantra, morning and night. As simple as it is, it will have powerful ramifications. I shared with you how I had insecurity and fear which were lifelong issues that trace back to my childhood. As I continue to repeat the mantra, the self confidence has grown. For the first time in my life, I truly feel confident, assured, mentally and emotionally healthy. My lack of self-esteem caused me to choose wives who had low self-esteem. With the ever-growing confidence replacing the fear and doubt, I am ready for great things going forward. God is working in me, using the bold statements of faith I keep repeating, morning and night, to work in me to do His will. He cares enough about me. He cares enough about you to work in you every day to bring about a glorious future for you. WOW. What a blessing. Praise the Lord! It starts with the simple first step, repeating the mantra day and night.

The repeating of the mantra is a daily step. So is prayer. Now that you have your battle plan, your prongs of attack, you need to start each day with prayer and invite God into these specific areas. Prayer opens up the door. You need to invite Jesus into each area of your life to work and to do His will. I end my morning quiet time the same way, on my knees asking Jesus into every aspect of my life. I pray for His power and protection in me, my children and loved ones, asking Him to cover me and my loved ones with the blood of Jesus - a hedge of protection. I ask Him to bring the opportunities in the three areas and give me wisdom to see the opportunities that He puts in front of me and to give me the courage to do the steps He puts in my path. Just invite Him in. That is all you have to do. Ask Him for wisdom. Do it every day asking SPECIFICALLY in these two or three areas to move and to guide and direct. Because you are focusing on these few things every day and inviting Jesus into your life to work in these areas, you will be much more aware of the opportunities. Then, just take that next step God opens up.

The two go hand in hand. As you start and end your day with the mantra, God is working in you. As you pray His wisdom and guidance DAILY into the prongs you have down, your areas of concern and giftedness, you will be more aware of the opportunities He opens up. As your confidence grows, you will find it easier to go through the doors Jesus opens. Every day you will awake with more joy, more confidence, more expectation of what God is going to do today in your life. Each day is a new adventure as you grow up and grow into a true partnership with the Lord - Him leading, you joyfully following. You don't have to worry about how it will all play out. You don't have to worry about the past, for you know God works all things for your good (Romans 8:28). Soon, His peace will grow in your life - the peace that surpasses all understanding. You just read your mantra and pray and obey and leave everything else to Him. This is what Jesus wanted for you all those years ago when He spoke through the ages "I came that they may have life, and have it abundantly" (John 10:10).

And I wish I could end the book right there with the phrase, "And they lived happily ever after." But this new life will not come without a fight. It is called a battle plan for a reason. There is a thief that is focused on your destruction and we need to understand the enemy we battle and his main tools and schemes so we can be aware and be ready. The entire verse of John 10:10 says this, "the thief comes only to steal and kill and destroy, I came that they may have life and have it abundantly." Jesus acknowledged that we have an enemy, his name is Satan, and he is a liar and a thief and he is bent on your destruction. He will come after you hard when you first get started with this new battle plan because he does not want you to grow in strength and favor. He wants to keep you side tracked and mired in defeat so you can have no impact. BUT HE HAS NO POWER UNLESS YOU LET HIM. In any battle, it helps to know the plans of the enemy. If you know what he is likely to do, you can be ready and have victory. In the next chapter, we are going to go over the main tools that this enemy will use to stop you. YOU NEED TO START THE MANTRA AND KEEP PRAYING EVERY DAY FOR GOD TO WORK IN YOUR PRONGS OF YOUR BATTLE PLAN. That is your main task. Those two things. Then, let the Lord lead, but be on your guard for the thief. Once you know his methods, you can see them for what they are and can overcome them with the tools Jesus has already given you. God is infinitely more powerful than the enemy, and He will give you abundant life if you just stay focused on Him and not fall into the tricks of the enemy.

My Thoughts on Chapter 4:

Chapter 5:

How to Overcome the Enemy

The biggest tool of the enemy is ignorance - ignorance from believers unaware of the enemy's influence in their life. Once you know the enemy, once you see how he trips you up, you can then be on guard for it and use the powerful name of Jesus to overcome it. But you have to be aware of his many tricks and schemes. Below, I will name the main ones I can think of. There are doubtless to be countless other ways that Satan trips you up. As I list the main ones, I hope you will become more aware so you can see the way he trips YOU up, and you can be ready for it with an answer. Again, he has NO ability to stop you unless you let him. You were given the power over Satan by Jesus at the cross. Satan can only stop you if you let him. So, let's explore some of his main schemes to keep you in bondage and bearing little fruit, and then we will talk about tools to combat these schemes.

FOCUSING ON YOUR PAST

Guilt over your past is a huge weapon for the devil. So much so that I want to camp out here for a while. So many believers are torn up over the mistakes they have made and every time they start to make headway, Satan is whispering in their ear, "You can't do that. You always fail at that." This happens usually at the first sign of failure. For example, you and your wife always seem to get in a fight over money. You have chosen to create a prong where you will "Glorify God in the area of money in my marriage." Sure enough, your first day implementing the strategy, your wife gets a call from your bank. You bounced a check. You get in a huge fight over it and hang up on her. Satan is right there, whispering, "See, you just are no good with money. You have never been good with it. You will never change. You can't fix this." Take my word for this, almost immediately after starting a new and powerful change, you will slip up in that area and Satan will pounce. You need to follow Jesus' model for dealing with the lying words of the devil.

In Luke 4, Jesus is led to the wilderness by the Spirit and fasts for 40 days. While there, the devil attacked Him with words just like he attacks us. Jesus was hungry, so the devil went after that weakness twisting Scripture in his words. Let's pick up the story in Luke 4:3, "And the devil said to Him, 'if you are the Son of God, tell this stone to become bread.'" Not only was Jesus hungry, and that was probably a tempting idea, he was also being tested in the area of pride. "If" you are the son of God… How many of us would have wanted to just turn it to bread to shut the devil up? Right? I mean, that would have been hard to resist, but that would have been playing into the devil's hands. In fact, if he did that he would be obeying the devil himself. Instead, Jesus modeled the way to overcome Satan's lies…with the Word of God. Jesus responded in verse 4, "And Jesus answered him, 'it is written man shall not live by bread alone.'" BAM!

How do you overcome the lies of the devil? With the truth of the Word of God. The Word of God is the sword of the Spirit (Ephesians 6:17). It is your main weapon against the devil and his lies. Let's go back to our husband with the money situation. When Satan steps in and whispers, "You have never been good with money and you will never change," the husband is there with the TRUTH of the word of God. He states, "I am a new creation in Christ and I can do ALL things through Christ who strengthens me." He may even want to pull out his mantra and repeat it right there. Satan will use your past. He will bring it up again and again. He will try to keep you focused on the past, the failures, and use it as the reason why you cannot be successful today. That is NOT Jesus whispering those doubts in your ear. That is the devil.

The first two chapters of this book were focused on the truth of who you are. You are made in the image of God. You are glorious. You are changed. You are a new man or woman. You are a new creation and your past no longer holds you. You prayed for God to remove the guilt, and He has forgotten it. Why can't you? You need to put the past behind you once and for all. Stop plunging up the past like a clogged toilet. Flush that stuff away. Stop apologizing for the mistakes you have made. You repented. You are free. Think of it this way. When you criticize yourself over your past mistakes, you are actually criticizing God. He made you, so your constant criticism of yourself is really criticism of God. STOP. Embrace the truth of who you are and stop the criticism, stop the plunging.

Know that Satan is going to use this technique, over and over, he will use every person, every situation, every tool he can to convince you that you are your past, that failure is inevitable, and you will never fix this problem. All of it is lies. You need to choose a Scripture that specifically counters that and repeat it immediately when the first lie appears. You need to be ready to answer that lie with the truth of who you are in Christ and how your future is assured not by you or your skill, but by Jesus himself who will guide you step by step to that glorious next level. There are some other things we can do to strengthen ourselves which I will go over in a minute, but know that this area will be a focal point of the devil. He will attack you there. Be ready with the almighty word of God

OTHER PEOPLE

The enemy will use other people to trip us up as well.

We must be on our guard against this. The truth is, some people may need to fall out of our life if they will only limit your walk with the Lord. This can be hard to do, and you may argue and say you want them to grow as well. If certain people consistently lead you astray, they need to fall out of your life…at least for now. Maybe down the road God will tell you to step back in and minister to them but for now, obey what God tells you. Be on the lookout for the times you trip up and if you trip up consistently after talking to a certain person or spending time with a certain person, be aware of it and maybe avoid that person for a time. Ultimately, ask God for wisdom and He will reveal the step you need to take. Don't be surprised if He asks you to put away this or that person from your life for now. Be aware that some people can harm you EVEN THOUGH THEY DON'T MEAN IT. Many people have been led astray by well-meaning people. Be careful who you associate with.

Also, the devil may prompt other people to outright attack you. Listen, if you are gaining ground for God then you are taking ground from the devil. He won't like that, and people may attack this new you. Maybe your spouse criticizes what you are trying to do. I know if this book becomes successful at all, I will face criticism. It is a given. In fact, if you never get criticized, you probably are not doing much for the Kingdom. Jesus was constantly criticized by pretty much everyone. This was proof that He was doing things right. When these attacks come from those we love or the very ones we are trying to help, it can hurt. Here is where grace comes in. You need to understand, it is not them who is attacking and it is not you they are attacking, it is the devil using them to attack the things you are doing which have him scared. Don't listen to the criticism, put it aside. This is easiest done by showing grace. When the attack happens, model Jesus on the Cross who said, "Forgive them Father, they know not what they do" (Luke 23:34). If you can forgive them, their criticism cannot harm you any further.

FEAR

Man, fear is a killer. Fear is ALWAYS from the devil. Perfect Love drives out fear. God is love, not fear. I am not talking about reverential awe of God Himself. God is all powerful and we should respect that power, but that is respect for the Creator because of who He is - present tense. I am talking about fear of the future, fear of a situation, fear of addressing a problem, fear of how someone will react. All of these are not facts. They are limiting beliefs tied to something that has not even happened yet or things from the past. Just because you fought with that person yesterday does not mean you will tomorrow, and you should not be afraid of it. The type of fear that binds us has NO AUTHORITY in your life. You are allowing it, and the devil will feed it. Over my life I have only found one way to overcome fear - face it head on. Do the thing you fear, and you will have the power. So, you begin this new mantra and begin praying for these new prongs of your life to manifest and sure enough, doubt creeps in. Satan may use another person telling you this is stupid, or another person telling you that you cannot do this, or you just start talking to yourself and telling yourself the same excuses you have used in the past. STOP. You must resist the devil. James tells us, "Resist the devil and he will flee from you!" (James 4:7).

As soon as the fear starts rising up, whether it is from the little lies of the devil, from someone else bringing it up or from your own negative self-talk, you need to stop. Hit the brakes, and again, speak truth into the situation. Listen, you are fearfully and wonderfully made and all power has been given to Jesus and you are given that power by the authority vested in Him. There is NO reason to fear. God tells his people over and over in Scripture "do not fear." He told Joshua. He told Isaiah. Find a Scripture verse that addresses fear and hold it near and dear, and as soon as fear raises its ugly head, speak truth into it. I love Isaiah 41:10. Psalm 56:3 is good. Philippians 4:6-7 are good. In John 14:27, Jesus specifically says, "Do not be afraid." And on and on. So many Scriptures. Pick one. Then keep it handy for when the fear creeps up. Fear has NO place in the believer's life. The devil has NO power here. The only power he has is what you give him, so don't give him an inch. As soon as fear creeps up, squash it with the word of God. Then move forward boldly with what God is telling you to do.

DOUBT

Another huge tool of the devil is to create doubt in your mind over the steps God has given you to take. I get asked this question all the time. "How do I know it is God telling me what to do?" or "How do I know it is God's Will?" In fact, I get asked this so much that I feel God must want me to address it in this book, and it is an excellent question, so let me try to address because it really can be tricky. God speaks in the small still voice a lot of times but what you need to realize is that Satan also has access to the spiritual realm. He can use the small still voice as well. SO how do you know it is God you are hearing and not the devil himself? I use a simple three step method to determine whether this is God speaking or not.

The first step is this simple test - Does it mesh up with Scripture? God will NEVER tell you to do something that violates His own word. God can NOT be where sin is, He is holy. If you are in a place of sin and are hearing the small still voice telling you to do something, that very well may be the devil.

You are married, but you are on the lake with a beer and enjoying the sun while the man you are interested in is driving the boat. You feel sure that this is the life you were meant for. You feel it in your soul. You are so at peace. You are sure God is telling you to leave that husband. That is not God you are listening to. God will not be there talking to you in the middle of your sin, encouraging you to divorce your husband. That is not God. Those are Satan's whispers. God would not tell you to divorce as He hates divorce. That violates His word, and you can be in a good place and still be whispered to by the devil. I have seen many people divorce their spouse and leave them for someone they met at church. They felt sure that God was telling them to divorce and they used the fact that they met at church as their valid reason. Again, God will not speak into your life and tell you to do something that He clearly says in Scripture not to do.

I don't want to pick on any one sin. It can be anything. Someone wrongs you and you feel like you need to "let them have it." That is not God telling you to react in anger. God says to turn the other cheek. Now maybe God does want you to address the situation, but He will tell you to address it with love and concern for the person. God hates the sin but He loves the sinner. The person is still made in His image. He or she is a child of God. And if God is telling you to address something with them, He is going to want you to do it in love. So, when you feel prompted to do something, the first check is to see if what you are being told to do matches up with Scripture. Not just one little verse of Scripture, but the general canon of Scripture. This is why it is important to continue to learn and grow. The better you know Scripture, the quicker you can react properly when God tells you to do something. If you are not sure if what you are being told to do is lining up with Scripture, go to someone who you respect as knowledgeable and seek their advice. For me, I go to Bill Prince when I am unsure. The world is black and white to Bill Prince and it is beautiful. If I am contemplating doing something and it is not matching up with Scripture, Bill will just say it. "Well Brian, that is not what the Bible teaches." Ugh.

This is where the rubber really meets the road. The problem most of the time is we know what God wants us to do, but we want to do something else. We want to support our decision, and we will seek out people who we know or we think will tell us to go ahead. The man who wants to cheat on his wife will call up his friend who is married to the woman with whom he cheated. He won't call up the pastor who has been married to the same woman for 30 years. What is really happening is we are trying to be on the throne of our life. This is not doing the steps God is telling us to do. This is us FIGHTING the Lord. Never a good idea. If you seek out someone to help you see if what you are being told lines up with Scripture, don't look to sympathetic friends. Look to the strongest believer you know and get their opinion. If you are not sure, email my friend Bill Prince at Biblical Principles, Inc at info@ biblicalprinciplesinc.org. He will shoot you straight. One of his main ministries now is counseling people over the telephone or email, and he welcomes those opportunities. Give him a try.

So what happens if the thing you are being led to do lines up with Scripture, and yet you are still hesitating. The next step is to try to find out why. IF you are hesitating because you are afraid to do it, or afraid of how this will turn out, then it is likely that you need to move forward with it trusting the Lord. Remember, fear is from the devil. You have nothing to fear. If you are afraid to do something that you think God is telling you to do and it lines up with Scripture, then it is likely that this fear is just the devil trying to stop you. As we discussed a minute ago, the way to overcome fear is to move forward boldly trusting in the Lord. If it matches up with Scripture and the only reason you don't want to do it is because you are afraid of how it will be received, I tell you that you probably need to go ahead with it. That is likely the devil just trying to keep you from obeying the Lord. Now, what if it lines up with Scripture, and you are not afraid of the consequences of the obedience, but you are still unsure? Then in that case you need to just stop and pray.

That final step is take it to the Lord. And you may have to pray over it for a few days until you get clarity from the Lord. Be careful. If the reason you are hesitating is you really want to do something else, you need to take that to the Lord. Ask Him for wisdom. He says in His word that if we ask for wisdom He will always give it to us. Pray for Him to give you wisdom and peace about the situation. Just make sure you are not stalling because in your heart, you want to do what you want to do. That is sin and will never work out for your best interest. Come clean before Him and ask for His will, not yours, to be done. As you pray this way, He will give you absolute clarity. Then, move forward with it trusting that He is going to work it for good. Don't worry about the initial response, your job is just to be obedient. You have no idea what God is up to and how He will work it out, so just trust. Move forward with boldness and obedience, and leave the results to God.

OUR THOUGHTS

Negative self-talk is a powerful tool used by the devil to keep us down. People don't realize how powerful their thoughts are. Many people have spent their whole lives telling themselves that they are not this or that, that they cannot do this or that, that they are not worthy, etc. THAT IS THE PURPOSE OF THE MANTRA. It is to counteract our negative thoughts with new powerful thoughts. Jesus did not need a mantra because He KNEW who He was and why He came. His parents lost Him at 12 years of age and found Him in the temple. When they questioned Him, He said, "Did you not know that I had to be in my Father's house?" (Luke 2:49). Even at 12, He knew His deal, but we have spent a lifetime confused, barraged by negative people, thoughts and attitudes, and we have a lifetime of mess up there. We need to re-affirm truth and speak it over and over until we create new habits of positive self-talk. As you repeat the mantra, you will begin to grow in strength. BUT YOU NEED TO BE AWARE OF HOW SIN CREEPS IN. Sin begins with the seed of thought. The thought of sin gets sown first. Then, when it conceives, it becomes sin. When the sin is acted on, it becomes death. The devil will work to give the sin a place to get sown.

Here is a married woman, trying to set up a single man with a woman. It doesn't work out. She sets him up with multiple women but they never seem to work. The husband sees this, thinks it is strange that she is trying to set up this single guy with her girlfriends but doesn't put too much into it. Six months later, this single guy and this married woman find themselves all alone in a place, and a kiss is born. They will swear it "just happened" but somewhere in those six months the thought became lust, and the lust found an avenue to become sin. That sin ultimately led to the death of the marriage and the breakup of a family. And it all started with a thought, months before the sin actually happened. SIN ALWAYS STARTS WITH A THOUGHT. It NEVER "just happens." Guard your mind. Guard your heart. Be aware that the sinful thought will bear fruit if you do not squash it. How do you squash it? The word of God and bringing the sin out into the light. If you are thinking about a sin, bring it out. Bring it out in the open. Let trusted people know you are struggling in an area and let them help hold you accountable. The disclosed sin has no power to keep you down, just the sins you are hiding. We are called to help each other. Accountability with good, like-minded believers is a powerful tool. Use it.

UNEXPECTED SETBACKS

Oftentimes, when you are on the cusp of big things in your life, unexpected situations arise that you could not foresee. Maybe you are just getting going writing that book and your father dies. Or you are just getting going doing your mantra and obeying God in the little steps and you catch a wicked virus that sidelines you for a week. These are all just temporary distractions. They are NOT reasons to quit. You just need to gird yourself up in prayer and keep moving forward. Handle the situation as best you can and get back on track. BUT BE AWARE. Maybe that setback is actually an opportunity God is putting in front of you to live out what you are being called to do. Remember, He can work ALL things for good. So, don't get down. Don't get sidetracked. Keep moving forward. Keep reading the mantra. Keep praying. keep building yourself up. Positive songs and sermons can be great ways to keep your spirits up as well.

These are some of the tricks and tactics the devil can use to knock you off course, but they can NOT stop you unless you let them. You have the power. You have the Lord. Let's talk about the tools you have to combat his tricks, and then you will be ready to go to battle to craft the life you always wanted

BATTLE WEAPONS

Thankfully, God does not leave us alone to fight the powers of darkness. He gives us lots of tools and instructions. We already talked about the power of putting away your past forever. If you truly do this, then many of the tricks of the devil like guilt and negative past memories get put to death.

Isaiah 1:18 - "Come now, and let us reason together says the Lord. Though your sins are as scarlet, they will be as white as snow."

Check out Isaiah 43:18-19. "Do not call to mind the former things, or ponder things of the past. Behold, I will do something new." This is a direct promise in Scripture. God promises you are not your past. He makes all things new.

The Word of God is the main tool or weapon. In Ephesians, Paul shares the powerful passage on the full armor of God. I encourage you to read Ephesians 6:10-17. Many sermons and books have been written on this passage so I will not belabor that point here. But I love Ephesians 6:10, "Finally, be strong in the Lord and in the strength of His might."

You are NOT alone in this. Jesus Christ, the all-powerful Son of God, mediates on your behalf. The Holy Spirit of God flows in you. You just need to let Him work in your life.

GRACE

There may not be a more powerful tool than grace. Grace for others, and grace for yourself. Listen, you are going to slip up. You can read the mantra every day. You can stay focused on your two prongs and pray hard each day and follow the Lord exactly and STILL slip up. Why?

Man, you are human. You are not perfect. I am not perfect. We never will be this side of Heaven. So, when you slip up you HAVE to give yourself grace. Don't start telling yourself how bad you are, how you will never do it, etc. God has made a way to reconcile us IMMEDIATELY. Just take it to Him and pray and repent. "Dear Jesus, forgive your servant for _____. Please strengthen me. Come into my heart. Keep me from sinning again. Grant me forgiveness Lord, and lead me forward in your strength and power." BAM! It is done. If you meant it in your heart, God hears your prayer and your sin is forgiven. You can rise up and get back to the work you have been called to do. That slip up need not be anything but a hindrance. You can drop to your knees right then and end it. You must give yourself grace. This goes for other people too. Others may say and do things that throw you off course. Just forgive them as Jesus forgave you. Give them grace and then you don't have to harbor the effects of anger which is just sin that will sidetrack you. Remember that you are not much different than them. You likely sinned just this morning, so have grace on them as you wish Jesus to have on you. Jesus prayed, "Forgive us our sins, for we also forgive everyone who sins against us" (Luke 11:4, NIV). This becomes easier the more you do it and is a huge weapon against the devil. The sins we do not release are the ones that hold us in bondage. Jesus came to set us free from that bondage. So, take it to Him…and be free.

With the powerful weapons of prayer, the word of God, and grace, you can overcome almost any scheme of the devil. These three things are powerful beyond measure. There is one other way we can gird ourselves for the battle and it is the practice of spiritual disciplines. Hey guys, we are talking about changing your entire life. A lifetime of bad habits and thoughts. A lifetime of defeat being turned into victory. The devil does not want this to happen. He is going to fight you until you grow too strong, and then he will flee and find an easier target. Especially when you are starting this new path, you need to be diligent in the simple daily disciplines that will yield victory. Listen, I am in sales, and I track the number of outbound calls I make every day. It is a daily discipline. I must "Nail my dailies." Meaning, I must nail my daily routines. What you are about to embark on is something MUCH bigger than sales success. You are embarking on life change. You will be attacked. You need to be aware of it and nail the routines and put around you the hedges that the Bible talks about. So, let's discuss these simple spiritual disciplines and then you will be ready to embark on your mission to change your world.

SPIRITUAL DISCIPLINES

Daily quiet time - Probably no other consistent thing has had a bigger impact on me then my daily quiet time. Mine is in the morning, which starts my day out on a good note, but yours can be whenever you find consistent time to spend one on one with God. Maybe it is at night as everyone is in bed. Maybe you break away for lunch and spend some time in the conference room with your Bible and prayer. The key is to spend some time every day with God, developing that relationship. For the believer, staying close to God is the most critical thing we can do. Jesus said, "I am the vine and you are the branches, he who abides in Me and I in him, he bears much fruit, apart from me you can do NOTHING!" (John 15:5). Whoa…nothing! The word abide hints at ongoing time with a person. It also is a constant help, encouragement, and accountability partner. If you are thinking of sinning, that time with God each day will convict you. When the first seed of that thought gets sown, going to God consistently will convict and ultimately help you stop before the thought becomes full grown sin. Oftentimes, that sin is preceded by someone falling away from church, from a consistent quiet time. The sinful seed of thought is being fed and they are running from the conviction of God. By staying consistent in that quiet time, you allow God to help you nip those sinful thoughts in the bud before they become actual sin that affects you and your loved ones.

IF a consistent time alone with God is a new thing to you, start easily. Maybe read a Proverb each day. There are 31 Proverbs, one for each day of the month. As you grow, you will dig deeper and deeper into the word. It will become live to you. One of the most amazing things to me is how the thing I read in my Bible in the morning, I experience later that day. It is as if God is guiding me to exactly what I need for that day. There is no real way to explain this other than God. The Bible is a living breathing book. It will help you TODAY with your problems of today. I can't even explain it. I am just in awe of it. Keeping a journal can be a great way to enhance your quiet time. Write down what you are learning and experiencing as you are experiencing it. This can give you great insights and growth. How you do it and when you do it are not as important as JUST DOING IT. Spend a little time with God each day and you will put a hedge around your life that is hard for the devil to attack.

Fellowship with other believers - "and let us consider how to stimulate one another to love and good deeds, not forsaking our own assembling together, as is the habit of some, but encouraging one another" (Hebrews 10:24-25). Listen, we need others. It is a lonely place to be if you try to do this life alone. The devil wants you to try to go it alone because you are weaker that way, but a cord of three strands is not easily broken. Fellow believers, both in a Bible based church and in your sphere of influence can be a constant source of encouragement, conviction, accountability and just an outlet. As I was going through the pain of the divorce to the woman I loved, Mary and Laurie in my office were a constant sounding board for me, listening to my junk and giving me insights. You need to seek out like-minded people and spend time with them.

Openness - Not necessarily a spiritual discipline in the purest sense but a powerful tool to counter the attacks of the devil. The undisclosed sin is the one that has power. Once you open up about your struggle to other people, some amazing things happen. One, the power of the sin is automatically lessoned, so much so that many times just disclosing it is enough to stop it. But it also allows others in. They can now encourage you specifically in your struggle. They can hold you accountable if you let them, and God can move in others to bring into your life the people and situations you need to cope. Additionally, you also open yourself up to be used by God to bless others. Are you thinking about a sin? Share it with a like-minded confidante and ask them to pray and hold you accountable. Don't forget the power of prayer.

OTHER HELPS

There are other helps that are available to every believer. In fact, we are living in such a great day and age. There is no shortage of helps. The smart phone is a world of opportunities at your fingertips. Struggling with something? You can download a sermon on that very thing. Then you can listen to it while you exercise or drive to work. Christian radio stations and songs are available with the press of an app. MANY times the words of a Christian song would be exactly what I was going through and the tears would flow. Man, the song "Even If" by Mercy Me[8] still makes me cry every time I hear it. Something about it moves me and that keeps us humble and focused on the author of that music - God Himself. No matter what type of music you are into, they now have good Christian music in that genre.

---

8   Mercy Me, *Even If* (Fair Trade/Columbia, 2017).

When you put all these things together, there is so much available to help you grow and become all you want to be. The devil has no power and authority and now that you know his tricks, you can be ready with prayer and the word of God. You are ready…ready to rise up to your new beginning.

My Thoughts on Chapter 5

Epilogue:

This Is Your Time!

You have your mantra. It is time to start the process. Begin your daily routine, morning and night reading that mantra. Each morning, pray God into the two or three prongs of your battle plan. Then go forth confidently, being careful to listen to the Spirit of God guide you to the next step. Then, with confidence and trust, do the step He gives you. Each day, just repeat the routine, worrying only about that day as Jesus said. Be ready for the enemy to fight you because he will. But you are ready. You know his schemes. You know he has NO power over you. You know what he will try to do to side track you. You meet his schemes with the powerful word of God. With prayer, and with Grace.

You start the process of a morning quiet time. You get into a group of like-minded believers and you spend time with them, growing and sharing and encouraging them as they encourage you. Day by day, your confidence grows. As the truths of your mantra work into the fabric of your life, you are growing as a man or woman, growing upward toward the Lord. As you pray each day in your prongs, God guides you each day to what you need to do. As you keep following the steps He lays out for you, it all comes together. Pieces move in your life that you cannot even explain and your life builds. Soon, you are impacting others and changing your world.

As you grow, maybe you need to tweak your battle plan. That is fine. You are a work in process. Just go back to this book and rework the plan. Don't be discouraged at the attacks of the devil or temporary setbacks. Give yourself grace and keep moving forward. Soon, it will be evident to all that a new man or woman is being formed, and as God finds you faithful in this place, He will begin to move you to greater places. A peace you have never known will settle on you as you come to realize you are smack dab in the center of His will and there is no better place to be. Fellow believer, your glorious future awaits. Time to rise up and change your world forever. I'm proud of you and I will be praying for you. Your time is now...

Documenting My Mantra

Documenting God's Battle Plan
for My Life

Documenting God's Battle Plan
for My Life

Documenting God's Battle Plan
for My Life

BRIAN PEART

CPSIA information can be obtained
at www.ICGtesting.com
Printed in the USA
BVOW06s1036241217
503608BV00016B/355/P